THE JOY
REVOLUTION

How God's Word helped to set me free

GW00480804

CARLA ECKHORST

Table of Contents

About this book

I remember being told by wise people in my church many years ago that whenever I felt afflicted by negative emotions it was without exception due to a negative thought I had been thinking. I knew they were right. At the same time, I was very aware that my own mind was on the other hand also capable of the most exquisite, beautiful thoughts.

This other mindset was so real, the consciousness of my own power and liberty so strong, that I knew beyond any doubt that the helpless, depressed, frightened person I presented to the world was not real at all. When I was in this radiant place, I knew I needed no one's compassion or help because in fact I was not lacking anything, I was whole, and excited to be me.

So, while I was trying to find how better to control what kind of thoughts my mind was entertaining in my everyday life, I was taught about the Bible. I learned that it contains God's promises to us, and that what it tells about Jesus' life is at the same time about me: showing me who

I am, what I have, and what I can do as a child of God. In other words, it is about my identity in Christ Jesus.

I was intrigued to hear that as children of the Most High we are meant to hold our heads up, to walk, think, feel, act, like someone who is aware that they are royalty, one of the sons of God. There was something in these thoughts that gave me hope and excited me, as they were new and revolutionary to me.

Thus began my journey out of my depression into joy. It did not happen overnight. I realised that I could not access these sacred truths with my ordinary brain, they would not speak to me. I needed to "come up higher", I had to have them revealed to my heart, to my spirit, by One who knew how to present them to me in a way that was perfect for me.

The Holy Spirit was ever ready to show me a Bible verse in such a way that it lifted me to a higher view and perception of myself or of a particular issue in my life; in just the way that was most likely to help me, or that I was best able to understand and embrace, because He knew what would speak to me and what I was ready for.

I would call the thoughts that thus came to me during long walks in nature, a co-creation between Him and me, my mind being inspired by the Holy Spirit.

Written over the course of several years, these pieces reflect my own development from the early writings as a "baby Christian" wrestling with my inner "demons" - and the style reflects the drama that it was for me at the time - via subjects where I deal with major events in my children's lives, to writings which are more peaceful, even playful, as I myself matured.

They really are mostly about relationships, born from my striving for peace and the right attitude in my relationships – with my family and other people, but also with my body and its health-issues, with nature, and above all with God; in some I address Him, in others He speaks to me. In many I focus intensely on a scripture, holding on to it and extracting from it anything that can help turn the tide, until the shift occurs, the switch in my mind to relief and joy.

I hope that my heartfelt love for God's Word will speak to you, the reader, too and change your possibly preconceived ideas and perhaps prejudices you may have against the Bible. I hope that, inspired by my examples, you will wake up to the spiritual truths that you too have access to, the revelation of who you are in Christ!

The exciting thing is that while there are, no doubt, countless different reasons why we are aching or fearful or hopeless, nevertheless the answer is One; and it is being offered us, tailored to our individual situation and need, in God's Word. In a nutshell, it is by allowing our mind to be elevated, lifted to the higher level of God's thinking, that peace and joy in the moment can be found, regardless of circumstances.

My message is that, once awakened to the power of their own minds in *practically applying* the truths they find, to themselves personally, readers would have a very realistic chance of shaking off their own yoke of depression; in fact, it is inevitable.

Dear joy

And he said unto me, My grace is sufficient for thee: for My strength is made perfect in weakness (2 Corinthians 12:9).

The very word "joy" sounds pleasant to my ears and writing about it seems a particularly wonderful task. It is the emotion I want and value most and the one I long to share with those I love. It seems to me that when I am "in joy" I am in my natural element. When I am filled with joy I feel like I have so much to give and my openness and the very life in me know no limits. It is when I want to jubilantly tell the whole world that it is true, "in His presence is fullness of joy" (see Psalm 16:11), I am the living proof of it.

I ask myself, how come I feel like I have a special affinity to joy, as if it is my field of expertise? This is especially interesting when I consider that, depression – the ultimate lack of joy - is the problem I have been afflicted with most of my life. Am I not rather an expert at heaviness and discouragement? You might ask, who am I to even begin to talk about joy?

And yet, it appears to me that being familiar with the deepest of misery, I am therefore especially qualified to recognise the joy that is the antidote to it. It is a joy that is more than the delight about some particular event or achievement like say, having won a sporting match, seeing your loved ones succeed at something, overcoming a challenge. It is more even, than feeling loved and appreciated by others.

Maybe it is because the more intense and unrelenting my misery, the more sensitive I become to recognising the light? At the same time, I am more willing to bypass the world's distractions and embrace the experience of being soothed by that which I consider the Most High.

Scripture says, "Don't be dejected and sad, for the joy of the Lord is your strength" (Nehemiah 8:10 NLT). The joy of the Lord is unlike what we settle for in this earth, it is independent of circumstances, is above and beyond the changing conditions and happenings we see. Nothing necessarily needs to change, but seen through the eyes of joy, there is abundance of beauty and reasons for gratitude everywhere!

Amazingly, as with the "peace of God that passes understanding" (see Philippians 4:7) there is no logical reason for this joy either, it defies human understanding. And yet it is all-pervading, inside and all around. It is dependable enough to share it and give it away and it causes me to step out and be courageous where in the past I might have held back, fearfully. Most importantly, it lifts me up, brings me up to a higher level of perceiving and functioning.

You may wonder how can this joy of the Lord be someone's "strength", when the maintenance of their mental health is their greatest struggle? I do believe that where we are the weakest God can show himself the strongest. I can confirm from own experience in more than one area that where I can do nothing in my own strength, I am more likely to be receptive to the grace of God; and where our need causes us to depend on His grace, it is here that we can have the greatest breakthrough, again and again.

Therefore, I can say with perfect conviction that joy, rather than being elusive and impossible for me to attain, is in fact my strength, my speciality, my favourite - the emotion that allows me to feel one hundred percent at home in my Father's presence.

In Him I live!

For in Him we live and move and have our being (Acts17:28).

Something in me already knows how precious these words are to me personally; this verse speaks to me again and again. To live, to move and to have my being – I love it, I cannot think of anything more beautiful.

For me, my depression always felt like being dead on the inside. This seemed to happen to me especially in the company of other people, I felt myself fading away, giving up, closing down. I regularly felt like I was being reduced to a shadow of myself, going through the motions until I had just enough energy left to drag myself home and hide myself and my shame from the world. For decades, this was my particular brand of depression.

That is why I learned to latch on to any scriptures speaking about life. The incorruptible life of God – a life that remains radiant, strong and vibrant, regardless of circumstances. God's own life on the inside of me, what could be more precious, and at the same time more real and insurmountable? What is there to fear when I am the carrier of this life? I began to understand that this Life within me is the key out of my prison. Every moment spent in remembering and meditating on the fact that "in Him I *live*" is a step closer to my permanent release from my darkness.

"In Him I move." I believe, another feature of a depressed mindset is the feeling of being stuck, unable to move forward, to make progress. I used to be so frustrated about my own self-defeating patterns, could see them alright and talk about them, but did not know how to move out of them. This has changed. Now that I am in Christ, I *move*. My life is going somewhere. When I remember that God is working on me and in me all the time, I feel a quiet gratitude and confidence; sometimes I am positively excited that I am not the same I used to be a year ago, and I will not be the same in a couple of months. How priceless is this for someone who has been going in circles for decades?

"In Him I have my being." Again, this has always been a desire so close to my heart, because all my life I have been longing to take up space and expand and express myself. It was always like there was not enough room for me to "be". The permanent sense of guilt I had years ago was somehow rooted in feeling bad for who I was; or, to be more precise, for *not* being me, but instead being so far removed from who I knew in my heart that I truly was.

Yet in Him, in Christ, in the "width of His love" (see Ephesians 3:18) I have space, I have my being, all of it. I can safely unfold and find it is not a struggle at all, there is no one to "protect myself" from or compete with. Instead, there is the joy of discovering who I am in Him, and, as someone put it, it is "a soft melting into Him".

Let me add here also, the simple act of saying "Praise the Lord", saying it to Him and meaning it from your heart. This includes singing worship songs as well. The amazing thing is, it makes *me* feel more worthy and valuable. I feel genuine when I sing "I adore you". As I realise that my love for God is real, heartfelt and profound, I know in my heart that I am not a bad person; I am loving and lovely after all.

If I can touch His heart and bring Him joy with

my love and praise, if He values my simple honest affection this morning, then I am glad to be me. I cannot live in the consciousness that I am bringing Him pleasure, that my praise is sweet to Him, and at the same time be depressed! These two are mutually exclusive. Thus, loving God helps me to love me.

Gladness poured all over me

You love righteousness, uprightness, and right standing with God and hate wickedness; therefore God, Your God, has anointed You with the oil of gladness above Your fellows (Psalm 45:7)

Yes, I do love the core of righteousness, the eternal truth of who we are in Christ. The purity and loveliness that cannot be lost or destroyed or in any way defiled. We thought we had to earn it, work for it, suffer for it – while it was freely given to us, His most holy blamelessness and innocence; it is ours by virtue of being a child of God.

To claim this truth, to be so conscious of it that we can simply *be* it, is what I believe we all long for; it is the greatest happiness. Having a glimpse of it is what makes me jump and dance and laugh for joy, it is such a relief, it brings tears of gratitude and gladness. To be aware of the dignity of my spirit self, which is who I truly am in Christ, is what I wish for myself and for all those I love. To see it in each other is the most beautiful gift we can offer.

And yes, I love uprightness. Being upright in the face of obstacles and unfavourable circumstances or strong opposition; staying upright despite discouragement, fatigue, self-doubt; despite old internal demons raising their ugly heads; I like that. Upright not so much in gritting one's teeth and struggling on, and putting up a fight, but upright in thinking right, in refusing to believe old lies about myself, refusing to stay down when I have been knocked off my feet.

It is a determination to keep coming back, over and over, to the truth, the light, the good news about me and my life, to keep reaching for better-feeling, happier thoughts. It is also patiently reminding myself not to dwell on what I do not want, to forego the temptation of the drama, of justifying myself, of being right, being understood, or whatever it may be. I love it when I succeed at giving my attention to the shining, joyful truth instead. That is the kind of uprightness I want to stand for.

Right standing with God – to me it means standing in agreement with his loving view of me, standing in the place where my heart's desires have already been fulfilled. It is where my mind thinks in line with the Holy Spirit who knows the truth about me. It is where I am open and ready enough to easily acknowledge and receive all the blessings that are held out to me. Where I am inspired, awake, enthusiastic about life, full of energy – all of this is the natural by-product of being in "right standing". Who would not love it?

I love all this and am not attracted to negativity, which is what I think the above scriptures' "wickedness" refers to. I do not get a kick out of negativity, it does not thrill me. I do my best, I hope to learn and practice, not to think about it; but keeping my mind on what is true, honest, pure, lovely, praiseworthy… - as we are instructed in Philippians 4:8. When I dwell on the opposite, I am no longer "in right standing". I know what delights me, what makes my heart sing, and when my heart is in the right place, I have access to all this gladness.

I am glad when I am aware of the loveliness and purity of my own spirit nature and of those around me, I strive to be ready to receive and give the gift of that awareness, even if it means overcoming resentment, or fear.

I have this sense of gladness and I love it when I keep coming back to the uprightness of light and happiness no matter what thoughts are pulling me down; I like myself and have hope in life when I am willing to practice the discipline of doing that, over and over again, regardless of how often I keep failing.

To me, right standing is where I feel like there is a beautiful purpose to my life, the purpose of being glad and rejoicing.

My gladness is poured all over me, like oil, it is precious, golden, smooth, nurturing and beautifying. Like oil, it makes smooth again what was brittle or creaky, and what was lustreless is made shiny; it brings out colours that may have begun to fade, preserves them and makes them more vibrant. It seems that gladness, like oil, is precious and gives life to what is beautiful.

In the Bible, kings were anointed with oil, I believe being anointed is an honour. The oil of gladness is elevating me, symbolizing my calling; what if it is my purpose and calling to be glad?

In my opinion, this sense of relief and lightness, this gladness is really all that matters, and the one ingredient in my life that I have always desired above everything else. I believe it will be my gladness that will speak more clearly to those around me than any of my words, it is what can give hope to another's tired soul. Let me live in gladness, be a champion of gladness, a smiling example of what God's Word says about us.

Heavenly Father

As I started my prayer with the words "Heavenly Father" yesterday, I pictured Him who cares for me with the affection of a father and whom I love with the love of a child, thinking of Him in His heavenly Kingdom.

I like thinking about His Kingdom. I picture it as a place of radiance, glory, and light, where conflict and fear are non-existent. When I meditate on it for a while I can feel intense emotions, experiencing it as the place I adore because it shines with harmony and beauty, so much so that sometimes it brings tears to my eyes. It is the place of escape from the contradictions and imperfections of this world, offering perfect peace.

In God's Kingdom I am one hundred percent free; I value this freedom more than anything else; it is where I walk in the glorious freedom of the sons of God (see Romans 8:21). It is the home of the intimacy, sweet closeness and love that have healed every wound and dried every tear. Sometimes the desire to be there has been so intense that I was ready to drop everything here and leave this world today, if I had the chance. There was a time I longed desperately to be there instead of here!

Then I was granted a beautiful thought. I am not meant to see myself as someone who, by being born in this earth has been deprived and disadvantaged, who was once the daughter of the Most High, a spirit being, and is now condemned to live in misery and lack. If I consider myself limited by my earthly existence, cut off from my true status as a son of God, I am believing a lie. No wonder I felt depressed; or at the very least restless, incomplete, as if something was missing.

What causes the pain is the longing for my true identity. That is why I was haunted by a sense of needing to get out of here, so I could BE.

Neither shall they say, Lo here! or, lo there! for, behold, the kingdom of God is within you. Luke 17:21

I remember during my first year or so, I used to cry every Sunday morning during worship. Now I am beginning to understand I am not meant to cry for home, as if I were exiled. I am not cast out or cut off. I need not wait to be allowed admission into the glory of the Kingdom, because it is inside

23

me. I am here to remember that I have never left my home, nor have I lost any aspect of the glorious liberty of the sons of God.

I am not under the natural laws of this world because I bring with me "the perfect law of liberty" (see James 1:25). The more I immerse myself in this law by studying what God's Word says about me, the bolder I will become in walking this earth with the right consciousness. I will be more inclined to remember that I am a citizen and ambassador of Heaven.

I am well on my way to understanding that there is no need for tears any more, for homesickness and pain, nor even for "Oh that we were there", as we sing at Christmas - for in our spirits we are there already.

Mount Leinster

Blessed be the Lord, who daily loads us with benefits, the God of our salvation! (Psalm 68:19)

When I first found God three years ago, I spent most of my time crying my eyes out on Sunday mornings during worship in church. I had so many emotional issues that needed healing, and false beliefs about myself that needed correcting. The tears were the result of all the knots that were being undone on my inside.

I remember how at one of the very first meetings my pastor told me that God wanted me to know that He loves me very much. I knew already then, that if I could truly grasp and understand this, I would never be the same. I knew it was the key, the answer to all my problems. I was wishing I could learn on the spot to continuously live in the consciousness of His love for me.

Recently, I heard someone speaking about the subject of joy. He quoted the Bible saying in John 10:10, "The thief does not come but to steal, and to kill, and to destroy. I have come that they may have life, and have it more abundantly." That spoke to me, in fact, it fascinated me to hear him point out that there is a connection between *have* and *enjoy*, the original word for these being the same.

I also liked the idea of having permission, even being invited, to enjoy life. There is nothing admirable or virtuous about not enjoying life! The Bible says that God created us for His pleasure (see Revelation 4:11). Like every loving parent, it must give Him pleasure to see His children live joyfully.

The speaker went on to point out the importance of enjoying all the details of our lives, such as our clothes, the food we eat, etc., because if we do not know how to enjoy the small blessings, how can we delight ourselves in spiritual ones? Most of my life, I rarely cared enough to enjoy anything, my perfect excuse being that I had no time. Yet in truth I did not know how. No wonder I was always depressed.

I thought, yes, he is right, I should really make an effort. Especially since I had been stuck in a fair bit of self-pity and negativity over the last while.

Amazingly, the next speaker I heard also spoke about the importance of enjoying our life. She said we need to *choose* to live joyfully. She was right: it does not happen by itself. We have to make the decision, every day, that we are going to enjoy life.

Recently, several people had been telling me about their outings to Mount Leinster in Co. Carlow, and how they had enjoyed that. It being a radiant sunny autumn day yesterday, I felt it would be lovely to go there, and when I could not find anyone to go with me at such short notice, I decided to go on my own. In fact, I enjoy going for walks by myself, do so nearly every day, as during this hour of walking and meditating on the Word I generally find new calm and strength.

Mind you, the climb up was a lot more strenuous than I had expected, the road going up and up, relentlessly, with hardly ever a stretch where one could take it easy. I was puffing and panting fairly soon. It was quite a workout, and I doubt I would have been able to engage in conversation with anyone, because I was so preoccupied with the physical struggle of the climb!

Whereas the fact that I did reach the top of the mountain was a success, and I had reason to be proud that I had not given in to my desire to give up and turn back, I also knew that I had not really enjoyed any of the scenery and views. I was far too driven and impatient to get to the end of this climb and be done with the strain.

I made the decision that I would make the most of the walk back down. I wanted the serenity and renewal of my mind I often find when during my walks I focus on God. Scripture says that He daily loads us with benefits (see Psalm 68:19). If that is so, then the very least I can do, is notice some of those benefits.

I began the descent down Mount Leinster. This time, I wanted to enjoy every minute of it, and be close to Him. Somehow, my heart remembered what to do: I made room for Him, acknowledging His presence. Just like I do during praise and worship in church. With practice, it has become easier for me to consider that He is right here, waiting for me to turn to Him; allowing Him to embrace and fulfil me, in fact, spoil me; and is that not what we all crave – someone to *spoil* us?

We were now walking together. He would point to different things and say, Look! Do you like it? I did that for you. And I would say, You did that for me? Oh, that is so sweet of you, thank you so much. That is beautiful, you did that so well, you are amazing! He would be pleased that I liked His creations and draw my attention and open my eyes to even more wonderful sights, and I admired things I had not even noticed on my way up.

He showed me some rocks He had sprinkled there, and I smiled at the thought that God can sprinkle rocks, just like that, for the fun of it, and I was glad to sit down on one.

Lower down, when we were no longer engulfed by chilly clouds, I noticed the sight of some vegetation, like a picture He had made, by playfully combining different colours. Some very fresh-looking bright green, it was moss I think, then a few patches of a darker green groundcover, and a patch of purply-red, and then, standing up and contrasting with it, the yellowy grey stems of dried grasses. The display of colours, radiant in the sunshine, delighted me. I thanked Him and said, You are an artist! And, like all artists, God likes His work to be enjoyed and appreciated.

There was water dripping in many places, and the grass and vegetation were covered in thousands of little drops. And God must have thought, Now I am going to shine the sunlight, like a spotlight, at such and such an angle onto this and show it to Carla, and she will be amazed - and I was!

Then He made me aware of the little stream of clear water running at the side of the road – I had not noticed any of it on the way up – so fresh and clean looking, I felt like drinking it, and I noticed the manyfold trickling and tinkling noises the water was making. So, besides sparkling in the sun, there were sound-effects added to the installation as well. I could see He must have had at least as much pleasure in creating this, as I was having now.

Do you like it, He asked. I love it, I said, thank you! And I meant it from my heart.

In order for my emotional issues to be healed and what I consider my "broken heart" to be mended, I need to make my relationship with God very real. His promise that He will never leave me nor forsake me (see Hebrews 13:5), the truth that He is *with* me, right now, always, has to be a tangible experience.

That afternoon was one beautiful experience on my journey, reminding me that I know the way out of my emotional torment. The battle with depression and negativity goes on, daily, but I am no longer powerless, I have the answer. I need to make an effort, yes, every day. Be honest with myself: Do I want to actively embrace the fullness of joy that is in His presence? It is not going to happen unless I make the decision. Staying in the Word and watching my thought life is utterly important.

And so are experiences like the above, because I am allowed to witness the joy in God's heart for being in relationship with me; with *me!* The experience showed me that my relationship with God can be still deeper and more real than it had been up to then; that He can be, and wants to be, everything for me, everything my heart yearns for.

It was the first of more experiences to follow, that touched my heart, because I am beginning to realise how boundlessly much He wants to give to me, how sweet He is! I have begun to open my heart more to Him and to enjoy loving Him back.

Dressed for Heaven

You have taken away my clothes of mourning and clothed me with joy... (Psalm 30:11)

Consider being clothed with joy. Wearing joy inside the house and when you are going out. Joy being the appropriate clothing regardless of where you are going, you will always look good and suitably dressed. Joy will be the right attire for any occasion, you will definitely leave a positive impression, possibly even inspire someone to look for a similar garment.

Joy will suit you well, underlining your beautiful features, there will be no need to worry that it will look wrong on your sort of figure, or for your age. You will not be judged; people will forget all about judging or criticising as they will be so pleased to see you.

Neither will joy be in any way uncomfortable or ill-fitting. You will not feel too hot in it, the sun will not burn you, nor will it ever fail to protect against cold, wind or rain. You will be perfectly sheltered and covered from head to toe, no matter where you go. It will never look worn or faded or unfashionable, but always be perfect. Knowing that you look your best you will feel confident, the smile on your face everywhere you go complimenting the joy you know and carry so well.

You are not wearing this garment to hide any aspect of you. On the contrary, wearing nothing but joy, you see your own beauty and perfection, which is showcased rather than veiled. You are at peace with all of yourself, feeling gratitude for how you are made. You are not dressed in joy to hide your nakedness, your shame or guilt or fear. There is nothing to hide. You have never felt so transparent and open and yet so dignified, innocent and safe.

You feel infinitely wealthy wearing this joy, knowing where it came from, how heavenly, untouchable and superior it is. And yet being so preciously attired does not make you in any way intimidating or haughty. On the contrary, people are drawn to you, just as you are drawn to invite them to partake of your joy.

The most important thing is that to wear joy, you must be more than a body. Joy is one of the fruits of the spirit (see Galatians 5:22)! When you wear nothing but this joy, you are therefore truly you, a spirit being, unlimited by any bodily concerns, way bigger than the tiny mortal frame of your body. If God has taken away your clothes of mourning - your consciousness of and belief in sin and death - and has given you His divine joy instead, it means that He considers you more than a mere mortal in a frail body.

It must mean that He sees you as a spirit being, worthy and capable to wear the sort of clothing worn in Heaven.

God's Word in my mouth

Then the Lord put forth His hand and touched my mouth. And the Lord said unto me, Behold, I have put my words in thy mouth (Jeremiah 1:9)

The Word of God is in my mouth. So then, I could imagine having the most precious things coming out of my mouth every time I speak, such as gold, diamonds, and gems of all kinds; or beautiful fragrant blossoms every time I open my mouth; or I could imagine my words as light, radiance. I imagine being allowed to use this most precious spiritual material to create absolutely anything through speaking it.

There is an abundance of it in me, at my disposal. Its presence in me fills me with joy, energizes me like a fire inside. I know it is a privilege to be entrusted with God's Word, and I treat it like a guest of honour inside of me. Just even thinking these thoughts creates a shift in my consciousness, makes me feel energized and worthy.

We know without a doubt that the Word has creative power, it is potent. That is why it is our victory over adversities. That is why we are instructed to declare it over everything, to speak it out loud, every day. It has a driving force inherent in it that adversity cannot resist. This power of the Word, released into the adverse situation, will cause results, accomplish what it says. It is dynamic, it cannot be deterred, it will not cease being active until circumstances have aligned with it. Is this not brilliant?

God's Word, being spirit and life, is also way larger than any problem, cannot be confined to the limitations of a complication. It already carries within itself the answer and solution to the difficulty, it simply overrides opposition, because opposition is insubstantial and inferior to the spiritual truth that reigns in the Kingdom. The Word does not need to wrestle with the adversity because it has already undone it.

With God's Word in my mouth, I am progressing. I am finally done with trying and with getting stuck. I have repeated the same old lesson so many times that I have finally understood there is no need to agonize and delay every time there is a challenge. No need to keep on wasting time going through the same old patterns any longer.

So, I choose the way forward. I say yes to God's Word in the first place. No more detours, reasoning, doubts, or any other kind of resistance. Instead, I go for it, with every fibre, no longer hesitating to embrace the truth, and to progress in life. Progress and success go hand in hand, and I know I am free to move forward and make my mark.

Nothing can hold me back because God's Word in me is the driving force. I begin to understand that I do not even need to make anything happen. It does not require my personal effort for God's Word to be effective. I do not scheme and plot and plan, I just get out of the way and respectfully allow the will of God to be accomplished, through me.

God's Word in my mouth will also allow me to grow in grace. To me, grace means the power of the Holy Spirit, and God's favour. It is given with so much love, so abundant and it is not willing to withhold any blessing from us. It is only our own slowness in accepting and feeling worthy of His grace that hinders God from introducing us to all that is contained in it. It is almost like we can only receive a teaspoon full at a time and are scared at the vastness of the ocean of all that His amazing grace implies. It is like we dare not look and consider that His grace has touched and lit up everything that concerns us.

The scripture enjoining us to grow in grace also says to grow in the knowledge of God (see 2 Peter 3:18)

With His Word in my mouth, I begin to recognize Him. I will know what is of Him and what is not. I will sense when He is present, just like I would recognize the voice of a loved one. The more time I spend with someone, the better I will get to know them. I will know what pleases them and what does not, what helps towards increasing the closeness of our relationship, and what disturbs it. All of this also applies to the relationship with God. The more often I find He is there when I turn to Him and the more often I experience His actual availability, the less likely am I to doubt His existence or discount His love.

Time spent with God's Word in my mouth and in my heart is time spent with God. It is allowing

Him to give to me of His life-giving thoughts. I permit Him to bestow His love on me through saturating me with His own nature. The joy in my heart will tell me that I am doing the right thing.

Ian's Story

Being confident in this very thing, that he who has begun a good work in you will complete it until the day of Jesus Christ (Philippians 1:6)

I have come that they may have life, and that they may have it more abundantly (John 10:10)

I woke up at some stage during Good Friday night 2010. My nineteen-year-old son Ian had not returned yet from the party he had gone to. I had learned long ago not to lie awake and wait for him since there was no way of knowing whether he would come home at all or stay the night somewhere. When at around 5 am a car pulled up outside our house I decided it must be a taxi. When the engine was switched off, I thought, oh no, don't tell me he came driving home! When I finally looked out of the window, I saw a policeman and -woman getting out, and my heart jumped into my throat. Opening the door to them, it was beating so hard I could barely breathe.

I was told very gently that my son had been involved in "a bit of a car accident" and was in hospital, nothing too serious, possibly just a broken leg. Seeing that I was in no condition to drive I was given a lift in the police car where I heard that Ian had been the driver and that he had "drink taken". My shock gave way to anger about this son of mine who had had already several brushes with the law, all stupid things he had done when drunk.

When I arrived, I heard him being addressed as Fred. For some reason he had decided to give them a false name, and the nurses, already tested by his loud drunken cursing and pleading for water, were not too pleased that all the blood samples had been sent off with the wrong label on them. I was impressed by their patience and good-temperedness despite my son's bad behaviour.

In the cubicle next to Ian lay Dan, who had been in the passenger seat of the car. He was not shouting, as I think he was unconscious a lot of the time. He had been very badly injured, with many fractures, actual bones sticking out of his limbs. This I was told by the third lad, who had been in the backseat and, amazingly, was uninjured and able to go home.

I was grateful just to sit there with my son who

was gradually sobering up, reassuring him that once his leg was operated, he would be allowed some water. Thoughts about the legal consequences to all of this began crossing both our minds.

The fractures were going to be dealt with in another hospital, and I guess we were waiting for the transport there, when both boys' complaints about pain in their abdomens led to the decision to give them x-rays. After an eternity of sitting with Dan's parents in the waiting room I was called into a small room and asked by the consultant to sit down.

He then told me he was very sorry to say that my son had a life-threatening injury to his aorta, the main blood supply vessel from the heart. Eight out of ten people would have died on the spot with such an injury and Ian would need to have a stent put into his aorta which was so badly torn that only a few threads were holding it together. The good news was that there was an excellent surgeon in Dublin who was specializing in just this kind of operation, and that is where my son would go.

This is where the battle began. Ian and the doctors were doing their part in the fight for his life, and for me it was time to rise to the spiritual battle that was raging unseen behind the scenes. This was an opportunity to put to practice everything I had learned since I joined my church two years ago. It was in this church that I met two passionate African women, "prayer warriors", so powerful, fierce even, in their prayers that it left me open-mouthed.

I contacted my pastors first, and the support I then received from everyone through prayers, texts and calls over the next hours gave me great strength. To know that all these people were speaking and proclaiming God's Word over Ian's life was powerful. Pastor Frank arrived in the hospital and "in the Name of Jesus" broke any dark assignment over Ian's life, spoke healing over his injuries, prayed Psalm 91, and the two of us agreed that Ian would live and not die (see Psalm 118:17). - A prayer of agreement between two or more people (see Matthew 18:19), using the Name of Jesus, and -most exciting- declaring God's Word, such as Psalm 91 – these are spiritual tools, weapons in fact, that we are called to use, and I hung on to them for dear life.

I had enough teaching in church to know that we are not meant to sit there passively and say, oh God, look how terrible this is, please do something. I was more than willing to believe He wants us to *use the authority* He has given us through Christ. The doctors were saying, we do not know if your son will make it, yet Scripture says we can be "confident in this very thing, that He who has begun a good work in [Ian] will also complete it" (see Philippians 1:6). I drew strength from the belief that, mixed with a sufficient amount of faith, God's truth will override the medical facts.

I was not unfamiliar with the idea that "you get what you expect" and was somewhat aware that my own negative outlook and expectations were holding me back from what I really wanted to achieve in my own life. Yet this was the time to radically change my thinking and expect a miracle.

The Bible said, I could say to this "mountain", meaning Ian's life-threatening injuries, "be thou removed and cast into the sea" (see Mark 11:23), and if I believed it in my heart, it would be done. Scripture also says we are given dominion over all circumstances by the power of Christ in us (see Romans 8:37). If this was true, why should it not include my son's situation? The key was, not to doubt. We had to stand in faith and "aggressively claim" those scriptures that were relevant to Ian's recovery.

I was immensely grateful to be allowed to go along in the ambulance. I noticed the driver's and the other medics' serenity and lack of panic and understood you cannot get too emotional every time you try to save someone's life. I was told how extremely lucky the two lads had been to have got out of that wreck alive. It was fascinating to travel so fast and see the cars in front of us scuttle out of the way.

All the while I was muttering under my breath all the scriptures I knew, thanking God that "all things work together for good" (Romans 8:28) and doing my best to fully believe what I was saying.

The long hours of waiting in the Mater Hospital that followed were way worse for my husband and our two daughters and their boyfriends than for me. I could see the awful fear, worry and tears in their eyes. All they had were the consultant's words who said that Ian's chances of surviving the operation were 50/50, and the kindness of the nurse popping in and out of the High Dependency Unit explaining why they are not operating yet and through her whole demeanour saying, look, do not hope too much.

Believe it or not, I had one of the most powerful and positive days of my life. That day I learned what faith is, and when mine grew weak and I was hit by fear and the desire to fall apart, I could lean on the faith of those in my church. I will never forget Pastor Miriam's words on the phone, "Have no fear." - It was as if I suddenly understood these words in my spirit, and I *got* it.

Another wonderful text message reminded me that on Good Friday, Jesus took all the injuries and bruising and mangling that Ian and Dan went through. He already died for them. It felt like a kind of revelation that struck me when I understood that there is absolutely no sense in them dying, suffering a death that Jesus had already suffered for them. Jesus died so that Ian and Dan should have life. And that they should

47

"have it more abundantly" (see John 10:10), not less abundantly, confined to a wheelchair. No, an even more abundant life than they had before all this happened.

Supposing that it is true that Jesus died so that we would never have to be defeated again by the afflictions of this world; what if I had insisted that this situation is far too serious and terrible? What if I had decided that after hearing what the doctors said, I could not see how something Jesus did 2000 years ago, could have any impact on my life or that of my family? I could have decided to try and make bargains with God instead, like Dan's father who promised God he would give up cigarettes if his son survived.

All of this would however have been equivalent to saying that Jesus died in vain, pointlessly. If Jesus' death and resurrection had the power to impact my son's life today then I had every reason to make the effort and *claim* what he died for us to have.

When the good news came that the operation had gone well, I shouted, see, I knew it! - before finally collapsing into a chair. On the way home we felt great, like we had just won the world cup.

The weeks and months to follow were not easy, and required a different kind of faith, a more sustained one. The adrenalin rush of that Easter Saturday was gone, and it was getting to me to see Ian looking worse every time we came to see him, puffed up after all his operations, feverish, and then very depressed when they weaned him off his morphine drip. Along with that, came worries about the legal and financial implications yet to be faced.

There were a few huge scares as well when at least twice it looked like Dan was not going to survive. Once he had fluid in his lungs and had to be rushed to yet another hospital, once there was bone marrow in his lungs. Another time we received news that his brain had been damaged (due to the high speed impact), meaning that when he was out of his induced coma he would have to spend a long time in a rehab clinic relearning the use of his limbs. In the end it looked like he would not be able to use one of his hands.

When I felt overwhelmed with worry and dread, I was calmed and strengthened in church where we proclaimed the Word over both of them. This was partly done in singing as well, and I will never forget the power and intensity I perceived in our common faith.

Today, both lads are fully recovered, their bodies fully intact, you would never guess they had been in the mangled car we had to go see in the scrapyard! The car had Dan's cut-up jumper still in it, as they were forced to cut him out of his clothes to get him out.

Looking back years later, I am still in awe at the long string of miracles we received by God's grace.

Not by might nor by power, but by My Spirit, says the Lord of hosts (see Zechariah 4:6)

The mirror of God's Word

For if anyone is a hearer if the Word and not a doer; he is like a man observing his natural face in a mirror; for he observes himself, goes away, and immediately forgets what kind of man he was (James1:23-24)

But thanks be to God, who gives us the victory through our Lord Jesus Christ (1 Corinthians 15:57)

If I really knew that I live in victory, then there would have to be an end to ups and downs. Then I need not be afraid of challenges, because the outcome of everything would be my victory. I would no longer think that even though in a previous situation I may have triumphed over adversity, there is no knowing how things will work out this time. I would no longer consider the possibility of defeat. It would then no longer be "realistic" to say it could go either way; because if I am a victor the outcome is victory.

Either I am a success, or I am a failure, but I cannot be both. If success is the life that God has ordained for me, then I have got to stop seeing failure. Then I must stop arguing with God about what I really am.

If I live in health, then I cannot be sick. The two do not go together. If God says I live in health, that is that. Then the symptoms I see must be delusions. If God's Word says I am healed and yet my symptoms make a lot of noise, trying to convince me of their reality, then I must be seeing something that is not there, looking at lies, having nightmares.

If God has given me both joy and peace as part of the life He wills for me, then the person who is depressed and conflicted cannot be me. I am not two different people living in the same body. God has not given me a split personality. My joy and peace come from the awareness of the glorious liberty of the sons of God, into which I have been translated. My joy is in learning who I am in Christ.

Through the revelation of God's Word, under the guidance and tuition of the Holy Spirit, I see who I am, and I see the transcendent life that God has ordained for me. This life cannot be worked out and planned for or predicted with my logical physical brain. It cannot be bought or enforced.

Nor can it be stolen from me. It cannot even be recognized with my ordinary everyday eyes. It can only be perceived with the eyes of the spirit.

Who I see in the mirror of God's Word is very much at odds and at variance with how I used to see myself all my life. What I see is such a relief, such an encouragement and so very exciting that I cannot get enough of it. It is like a revolution that has released me from prison.

I am very eager to look into the mirror of God's Word and keep learning about how I am so much more than the pathetic things I used to believe about myself. Looking into the "perfect law of liberty" (see James 1:25) - what could be more attractive! Now let me live in accordance with the picture of me that I see in the Word.

It seems ironical that today I found myself in a situation that brought me right back to a perception of myself that has plagued me most of my life. Not long after having all these revolutionary thoughts about the subject of righteousness, I went out into the world and had an attack of guilt with a fierceness I had not experienced in a long time.

Suddenly the idea of me being the righteousness of God (see 2 Corinthians 5:21) seemed ludicrous; the conviction of my own guilt, the consciousness of deep condemnation, were utterly overpowering. What is so dangerous is that in a moment like that I *believe* that I am bad, flawed, beyond any hope of ever being a clean, acceptable, loveable person.

Thank God I have learned to distrust all this seemingly powerful evidence against me. I know from experience that the only way out of this harsh perception of myself is to turn to those revelations of the Word that have spoken to me before. The goal is to get back to the conviction that what God says about me is true, that His view of me is correct.

It takes effort and willpower to keep asking for help, keep asking to be shown the scripture that will turn the tables, that will bring my mind back on track. In such a situation I need the revelation of the truth that speaks to my heart and brings back the joy and relief that enable me to forgive myself. Forgive myself for my little detour into old nightmares.

And suddenly the whole thing is much less dramatic than it seems. It was a slip, a little mistake about myself, that is all. Okay, I allowed the enemy, the spirit of secrecy and guilt, to have a couple of hours that I could have enjoyed without his interference; but he has not been able to change who I am in Christ, who I am in the mirror of the Word. I am no longer buying into the picture of me that he keeps holding up to me.

I could have acted a lot better in those situations today, in fact it is a shame that I did not. But the heaviness and destructiveness, the harm, the guilt, the drama that I saw in it and that devastated me so, are gone. They were the machinations of deception, illusions to frighten and discourage me. Now I can see them for what they were; and I am free, I am subject to the perfect law of liberty, not to laws made to condemn criminals to death.

This was no small feat. It is one of my triumphs over insanity and fear that are rooted in nothing more than a false picture of myself. This is an example of how I can *use* God's Word as a weapon in the battlefield of my mind. It is scary, it is far from easy, but it is possible, that is what counts. If

I have experienced it working once for me, then it is bound to work again, more times, as many times as I need. So then, there is reason for hope. I need not despair. There is a way. It is up to me to learn to walk it. I have been given weapons; it is up to me to use them.

I delight myself in what God says about me during my times of meditation; but it is during everyday life and interactions where I need to learn to apply them. They are for our practical use. We could call it practical Christianity.

I kept asking, what was it that You had taught me about my righteousness? I cannot remember, please show me again. Then it came back to me. I truly delight myself in God, I love Him, and I undoubtedly love His Word, I really do. So then, I cannot be a bad person, then I am of God. This memory was all that was needed for the switch in my mind.

I also remembered a scripture that had helped me in a similar situation of self-condemnation: I have been bought with a price! Therefore, I am clean now; and thus, the clouds lifted, the sun shone again, my sense of humour returned. I could see the beauty in my life, and all was well again.

Choose Life

Today I have given you the choice between life and death, between blessings and curses. Now I call on heaven and earth to witness the choice you make. Oh, that you would choose life, so that you and your descendants might live! (Deuteronomy 30:19)

I like that this scripture tells me of the choice I have between life and death. Sometimes it feels like what I do so often when I feel depressed is choosing *death*! It does not say that I should try harder to discover whose fault it is that I am feeling so low, or how to find someone or something that can make me feel alive, I am asked to choose life itself!

The first reminder here is that life will not just come to me, the awareness of my aliveness does not happen of itself. Life apparently needs to be chosen. If that is so, what can I do, how do I go about it? How do I get from feeling dead inside to choosing life? In order to be able to do that, I know a change has to take place in my mind first. Here I need to find the discipline and make an effort.

Though reluctant and unenthusiastic, I can at

least choose to meditate on this life that God has set before me. Finding that willingness is already a victory.

At the same time, I acknowledge that I have forgotten and that I need help to remember that it is life I desire, because in my depressed state, while theoretically I would obviously prefer to be joyful, I actually do not really care one way or another. For the depressed me, the memory that it is life I long for and desire, is out of reach.

It is almost as if first of all I need to ask for forgiveness for my state of indifference, before I can ask for help to be shown what it is I really want and love. As I allow the indifference to be cleaned off me by God's forgiveness, my honest request to be shown that life, is rekindled. I stay with it patiently, I know my spirit will remember my heart's desire, and the joy will return. As I remember life, I have already chosen it.

Hand in hand with it goes the realisation, once again, that I matter, and that God's will for me is to share in the joy of being alive. As these thoughts dawn on me, I begin feeling worthy again, oh what a victory!

Not only is life worth having, but I am worth having. I begin to remember that it is my own beauty and loveliness that enables me to see the beauty and loveliness around me. My eyes are open again, and I see colour and light, blessings and opportunities. I am back in the world of the living!

It is humbling too, that heaven and earth will witness what choice I make. My choosing life has an impact on my own current, earthly existence, which means the kind of day I am going to have, my physical health and my relationships; yet it has a greater impact still. The above scripture says it will cause my descendants to live; and I think maybe not only them, maybe others too.

The things I think and say, how I say them, the decisions I will make today, all of it is coloured by whether I choose life. It may have consequences for all life on this planet that are much further reaching than I understand.

Yet before the results of my choice can be witnessed on earth they are already witnessed in heaven; because my saying yes to life is a victory in the spiritual realm first, making heaven rejoice!

What a beautiful and, as I said, humbling, thought.

Meditation on a scripture like this enables me to snap out of my darkness and remember, once again, that I am in fact passionate about life. For me, escaping from the mindset that has agreed to an existence of differing degrees of misery is a miracle. It is a turn-around in my mind that I can and must receive *today*, as the scripture says, and every day.

Dwelling in me richly

Let the word of Christ dwell in you richly in all wisdom and spiritual understanding (Colossians 3:16)

For something to dwell in me, I need to let it in. I am grateful to have been taught and learnt that we must *take in* the Word, and that this can be done by meditating on it. The Word is like the food that nourishes us; some people go so far as to say, we must eat the Word! Once I have found the willingness, I devote time to thinking about a scripture, turning it over and over in my mind.

It is interesting that this is exactly what I do habitually with a problem; it seems normal to keep coming back again and again to a problem in the hopes of finding a solution for it. Now I am being asked to apply that mental focus in a far more beneficial and productive way. So, I stay with the scripture until I "get it". I know that this is the way I make it "mine". It becomes mine when I have understood it in my spirit.

Through meditating on the Word and allowing the Holy Spirit to reveal it to me, I reach the point where I agree with what it says, and I am off to a good start to the day. I have allowed the Word to change my mindset from seeing the world as an unfriendly place to seeing lots of possibilities and hope, from gloom to joy, from bondage to freedom, from dark to light.

For someone like me, who grew up with the belief in lack, the thought of having anything "richly", holds a thrill. I always considered myself as the one for whom there is nothing left, because I was sure there was not enough of anything in the first place, be it money, time, space or love. Something valuable offered me freely, an abundant supply, and all I need to do is just help myself to it, is a most unusual concept; and what a privilege it is!

Being asked to make sure I am so filled up with the Word that I am saturated with it: what a fascinating thought. Imagine eating loads and loads of food. We do not think that the more food we put on the inside of us, the richer we get. Yet we are asked to go after the Word with a "voracious appetite". This is something I cannot eat too much of; it will not make me overweight, but it will allow me to access the riches that have been prepared for me in the spiritual realm.

Those spiritual riches are waiting to be expressed and manifested through me in this world. We are told that just like a cloud, once it is saturated with moisture, will release it through rain, so we, once our thought life has been saturated with God's Word will begin to speak and act in accordance with it.

I love this idea of richness. My job is to keep up the intake of the Word and the renewing of my mind, because the old negative thinking is forever waiting and trying to steal and destroy the new life that has been planted. I believe and visualise how the sheer richness of the truth in me is crowding out the enemy, he simply cannot stay, cannot get a foothold, because there is no more space for him.

I know he will not give up because he needs me for his own survival, and without the cooperation of my mind he is deprived of his power; but the more real the Word becomes to me, the more unreal his threats become. He cannot hurt me, he may try to interfere with my circumstances, but he cannot decide how I view them.

The above scripture mentions wisdom. The

wisdom in God's Word is the beauty of it. This is why I love it. Wisdom can only lead to good, what is said and done under the guidance of wisdom will build up, strengthen, simplify, clarify, stabilise my life.

Yes, my spiritual understanding responds to God's Word. My spirit can understand and grasp the value of the riches that have been offered me; they are what my spirit knows, they are akin to my spirit's nature, suitable, compatible with it. They do not jar, do not require compromise. My own spirit can wholeheartedly say yes, give myself, connect with the Word, because it confirms my spirit's own nature. My spirit is thrilled to recognise what it has always known. This is where I am at home.

Finally, what a wonderful thought, having the Word dwell in me. That means I have a very special guest. What a privilege to imagine the purest, loveliest, holiest being, precious and unspoilt like a new-born baby, on the inside of me, carried by me: dwelling in me, and wishing to dwell in me, sharing its presence with me, considering me a suitable vessel. I want to live in that consciousness today.

More on joy

Therefore, with joy shall ye draw water out of the wells of salvation (Isaiah 12:13)

I believe the Holy Spirit is forever looking for possibilities to present to me the things he wants me to learn, different aspects of my life as a Christian that He wishes to bring to my attention. There is so much that He needs me to become aware of and understand; probably lots more than I can even imagine. Sometimes it feels like He presents a certain subject to me for a number of days in a row, or even longer; like for instance when the same scripture reaches me through different people or channels, as if it is holding out a special message particularly relevant to me at a particular time.

Then it is up to me to pay attention. Applying myself to it means turning it over in my mind, so that I take it in and let it speak to me, to the best of my ability. I begin to realize His keenness to show me how a particular teaching relates to the everyday affairs of my life. What is needed of me is my willingness to listen and learn.

Gradually I understand that there is an ocean of insights by which He wants to completely revolutionize my thinking! Every day that my mind is not available to Him is a loss, really.

One of these subject areas will always be joy, and there is still more the Holy Spirit has been showing me about it lately.

The above scripture speaks about the well of salvation. It is wonderful to have a well, especially if you live in a dry place, what a blessing! Yet the well will not be much good to you unless you draw the water out of it. The water will not come to you of its own accord, you have to want it enough to make the effort of drawing it. How tragic to imagine somebody sitting right next to an abundant well with an unending supply of water yet still dies of thirst because he does not avail himself of what is his.

Yet we probably all forget to draw as much of the water as we could and are meant to. Water is life-giving, it is indispensable, I sure need it and love it. The touch of water makes life spring up even in places where there was barrenness.

It is a beautiful symbol for the living water that

Jesus offers us! While in our western world it is so easy to get hold of water by turning on a tap, that we do not even think about it, the water that will quench the thirst in my soul needs to be drawn every day anew, by me personally.

So, how do I do that? The scripture says, with joy! Hardship and struggle are not mentioned in the scripture. Jesus has done the suffering, already paid the price. I believe joy is the key that enables us to access that which will give us life. I love this. Joy be to you all. Joy to the world!

Without guilt

There is now no condemnation to them which are in Christ Jesus, who walk not after the flesh, but after the Spirit (Romans 8:1)

How guilt-ridden I used to be. A lot of my actions, though on the outside praiseworthy and "right", were done not out of the conviction that this virtuous thing is what I wanted to do, but out of the fear of being blamed, found guilty, accused.

My typical conscientiousness, reliability and perfectionism, though perhaps laudable on the outside, were based on the secret fear of being criticised and found not good enough, the secret determination that I would not give the unloving world anything they could use as ammunition against me. So, while seeming to be such a "good" person on the outside, it was less an expression of my goodness than an expression of my fear of attack.

Now that I have embraced the righteousness of Christ all this is beginning to change. The escape from guilt, fear and condemnation is no longer the driving force behind my actions; because I *have* escaped.

What made the guilt issue so crushing and destructive was the way it poisoned my relationships and all my interactions. I believe the preoccupation with guilt can run in families and be passed from one generation to the next.

If you grew up forever heavy with the conviction of your guilt towards significant others in your life, you are likely to perpetuate that same consciousness in your adult relationships as well. You will project the parent that you used to feel guilty around, onto the people you interact with. You will not be able to even see the other person, because all you see is your own guilt. I can say all this, because I have been there, I speak from a lifetime of painful experience.

My delivery from guilt was not the result of my own superhuman efforts at proving anything to the world, it did not require becoming so perfect and having everything so completely under control that no one could ever hold anything against me again. It was given me as a gift, freely given as I embraced my new nature, my new identity in Christ!

It took me a while to understand what this "righteousness" which is of Christ entails. I am learning to grasp it in my spirit. The more convinced of its reality I grow on the inside, the bolder I get on the outside in opposing the old guilt pattern in my interactions.

This pattern manifested in habitually feeling bad because of something I saw in someone's facial expression that made me believe I had displeased them. Where someone in the course of a conversation with me, or any time afterwards, showed signs of fatigue, unwellness, or worse, depression, I would automatically assume responsibility for that.

This may sound ridiculous, but I can assure you it was no laughing matter for me: if someone would fall ill after being in my company, I would be utterly convinced that I had caused it. I guess the secret infantile fear at the bottom of all this was that someone might actually die because of me.

The revolutionary thing is this. My interactions are no longer devoured by guilt. Guilt is no longer ruling my life. It is no longer sitting on the throne, I am no longer its slave; because I know better now, I know the truth! I think its main weapon against me was appearances. It kept telling me to believe in what I saw, not in what I knew.

It insisted that anything and anyone out there had the power to change who I am, and whether I am acceptable or loveable. My identity was forever an uncertain thing, entirely at the mercy of circumstances and other people. If I succeeded in keeping someone happy, making someone laugh, I was "good", and guilt got off my back for a little while. If someone was not alright, however, I had failed, and this was cause for misery.

Now I know it is not my job to fix anyone else; their wellness and enjoyment is not the measure of who I am, and even *if* someone does not feel well after talking to me, that does not make me guilty. I have been trying to tell myself before, that if someone pulls a face it may be completely unrelated to me - and was hoping that it was so. However, now I know, even if their face *is* directly related to me, this does not make me guilty.

Maybe I have said something wrong, maybe I

need to apologize, but I am still beyond condemnation. I have not fallen from grace because I made a mistake. My loving nature has not been lost, because I may have been insensitive or inconsiderate for a moment. I can correct my behaviour as soon as possible, but I need not make this to mean anything about me. It definitely does not mean there is something seriously wrong with me. I am still God's very own workmanship (see Ephesians 2:10), there is nothing wrong with His creation, He knows what He is doing.

The new nature of righteousness also means that I am not doing anyone a favour by acting small, by seeking to boost others' egos by placing my own light under a bushel. If, according to God's Word I, as a son of God, I am the light of the world, well then I must shine. If I do not, for fear of upsetting anyone else, nobody benefits. There is no gain, no growth, no life in that encounter, or that relationship.

Embracing the Spirit that lives in me, and which is huge, does not make me an arrogant or uncaring person. I have been given a spirit of power *and* love, love *and* power (see 2 Timothy 1:7). They do not contradict each other. It is not a spirit of power and self-centredness, or love and inferiority.

There is no imaginary guilt I must pay for, nothing I have committed for which I have to pay another. My guilt has been paid for by Christ, once and for all. I need not continue doing penance by seeking others' approval of me, or by making everybody around me happy. If I have done wrong in the past, I will definitely accept accountability for it, apologize and make amends for it as far as possible. Yet after that, I am free to be what God has created me to be.

I will find that bringing gladness and ease to others happens of itself. Not by tiptoeing around them hoping not to dent their egos, but by being happy and alive myself. Instead of focusing on those around me, monitoring and seeking to control what is none of my business or my responsibility, I remember what God says about me. I keep my mind where it belongs, and that is the most valuable gift I can bring to any encounter or conversation.

The exciting thing is that God's Word prevails, it overrides all appearances, it is the "last word", no matter how much evidence to the contrary there seems to be. My perceptions cannot override what I know about myself. My perception can mean anything and nothing. I worship God in spirit and in truth (see John 4:23), and I have no confidence in "the flesh", in what my physical senses report about any situation.

The important thing is, once I have understood something in the spirit and refuse to take my eyes and my mind off it, it is bound to manifest in the physical realm. It is already here, and as I hold on to the truth that has been revealed to my spiritual eyes and disregard anything at variance with it, things are bound to line up with my vision. Situations will literally adjust, little corrections here and there, almost imperceptible, until everything reflects God's perfect will for me. All because I have put my trust in God's Word and have not doubted that it is already done.

Your Word is life to me

I call heaven and earth as witnesses today against you, that I have set before you life and death, blessing and cursing; therefore choose life, that both you and your descendants may live (Deuteronomy 30:19)

Dear Father, your Word is life to me. Yes, you are dear to me, even if day after day I keep on shutting you out of my mind and my heart, forgetting how much you mean to me, and how much you love me.

Thank you for reminding me that you have set life before me, for me to choose. That means life is not something that happens to me or that can be taken from me; it is your will that I choose it, it is right here before me, available now, always. It is the most precious, glorious gift I could ever want, because it is superior to any of my nightmares, no matter how convincing and insurmountable they seem. To me it is the life in which I find my victory.

And your Word, Lord, is the key into that life, it is the door, the way for me to enter into the realm where there are no limitations and where nothing is impossible. Your Word is the key to my freedom and liberation from all the complicated facets of my troubled mind, it is the answer to absolutely every unsolvable problem.

Your Word is what feeds me, nourishes me and builds me up; repairing what is broken in my soul and in my life, correcting and straightening what it is crooked and out of sync with how you see me. Teaching me who I am, whose I am, who my Father is, what I have, what I can do. Showing me the glory of the Kingdom that is my inheritance. How endlessly precious your Word is.

Oh yes, it is the light by which I navigate my way. When once again the world seems a terrifying place in which I seem unable to function; or when I have once again reached the point where I feel defeated, with absolutely nothing to lose, a broken person – it is then that the light of your Word is like a lifebuoy, a ray of hope that calls to me, encouraging me to pick myself up again, keep my eyes fixed on it and disregard everything else, just follow it, run to it.

Suddenly there is clarity and simplicity instead of the knots of complications and drama. And there is an opening to take my next step, "a path in the wilderness" (see Isaiah 43:19). While I have reached for that light in tears of helplessness, glad that a straw has been offered me, soon I feel joy rising at the light which illuminates the path ahead and confidence that I can safely set my foot on it.

And what joy to navigate my way in righteousness, victory and dominion! I have been made righteous, that means I am pleasing to you, I have the same nature as your Son Jesus. There is nothing bad, nothing evil about me. I have been freed from my habitual belief in inexplicable guilt towards everyone around me. Now I can smile and laugh with relief.

Now it is no longer inconceivable that I could have the victory over anything. Having your favour and love gives me boldness and courage. If you love and approve of me, then I can dare put my foot down. Strengthened and held up by your Word I can live up to your expectation of me and exercise my authority over the circumstances of my life. I am no longer a victim; and as I learn to triumph over my attacks of darkness, I know you want to teach me through your Word to function from that place of dominion at all times.

I cannot deny that I am most inclined to "give myself to the Word" when I am in pain. My soul is then like a field that has been ploughed, ready to receive the seed. It is true, that is the point where I begin to experience the prevailing power of the Word in my life.

The Word gives me a backbone that I did not use to have, an ability to resist adversity. This prevailing power props me up, gives me a strength that I can lean on and trust in because it is not of me. When you think of it, this is amazing. No matter how often I think I am back at square one, the power prevails, still working in me and for me.

And yes, the Word is transforming me. My mind, body and my life are no longer blindly conforming to the dreadful stuff I used to tell myself. No matter how many times still I am floored – still I can see that the greater and the more consistent the doses of the Word I take, like a powerful medication, the more obvious is the transformation that is taking place.

A miracle

But we all, with open face beholding as in a glass the glory of the Lord, are changed into the same image from glory to glory, even as by the Spirit of the Lord (Corinthians 3:18)

My diligence in studying God's Word and drawing close to Him, letting Him love and heal me, brought improvement in many areas of my life and reduced the fear in my interactions with others spectacularly, at times I really felt like a new and different person altogether. Yet certain core issues like the fear of rejection and hand in hand with it the fear of closeness, seemed very hard to budge.

A friend suggested that I should give my emotional issues to God. I was a bit confused, thinking that surely, He knew each one of my thoughts and feelings, so He must be fully aware of my suffering? Was there any need to "give" it to Him? And how? Had I not cried out to Him before, begging Him to *please* help me?

I had learned enough to know that He had

helped me already by sending Jesus to take all my afflictions, so that I would not need to bear them anymore. He had already taken my brokenness and given me His wholeness for it. Why then was I still suffering so intensely? For whatever reason, it seemed I was not able to *receive* His healing. I could claim my healing when it came to physical ailments, have come so far in regaining my physical health – but emotionally, that was a different matter; or so it seemed.

This morning, as I woke up with the familiar emotional pain, I gave it to Him, as best as I could I handed it over. I did not plead with Him to help me, nor did I try to escape from the pain by focusing on something else, not even by running to God's Word. The amazing change in my consciousness, that happened then is what I would call a miracle. My miracle for the day!

From pain to power, from victimhood to freedom: the heaviness lifted, and there was joy and lightness in me. It was like a revelation that of course I had received my emotional healing, that the healing had been going on all along. All the hard work and the time and the meditating on who I am and what I have in Christ had not been in vain.

I recognized that seeing myself as a wounded bird who would never be able to fly again, in a hostile, unloving world, was nothing more than a misperception that was not as impossible to lay down as it seemed. It was not holding me: I was holding *it*. It was a crazy old thought, nothing more. In truth, I have *long* outgrown it and left it behind me.

I had been experiencing many times how turning to the Word and meditating on what God says about me is like an antidote to my pain, that sometimes works instantly. No matter what shape or size the pain, once I had found the willingness to listen to the Holy Spirit and stay in that mindset, there was relief. I had learned that once I fellowship with the Spirit, I am free, I am not the broken person I used to be, I am free to shine, grow, expand into what He sees in me. The journey of claiming what I already am in Christ is going on and on, and it is exciting. It is from glory to glory, as it says in the Bible.

This morning I saw that I had been mistaken in believing that I can only be free and safe when I separate myself from human company, because somehow in their company my light gets snuffed out. I used to believe that I was just too sensitive and vulnerable to exist in this world; I do not fit here, and I do not want to be here, either.

My friend pointed out to me that God created me open and sensitive like that for Him, so that I might be receptive to *Him.* It was never His intention that I should be hurt in any way. I took to heart, especially as a child, anything thoughtless and uncaring that was said to me or about me in my past, while others might just shrug these things off. But I also took God and His Word to heart, and that is what He wants me for.

This morning, having given Him my nightmare, I became ready to accept, that the light and strength that I have as a spirit being does not turn into an illusion as I walk and exist in this world. I am not suddenly stripped of all that is mine in the Kingdom the minute I relate more closely to another person. That would not make any sense at all. This morning I saw that I have been built up and nourished and fortified lavishly in my spirit, and all I need to do now is spread my joy in the world.

Love affair

I cannot tell you how much it means to me that you think my love is sweet.

The ultimate love affair is the one I have with God. I think many people secretly believe themselves to be unlovable, I do not think I am the only one suffering from that. I have something else added to this though: every so often I berate myself for being so out of touch with my heart, feeling not just unlovable but *unloving.*

All the while God is knocking on my door in many ways; by giving me a Word, a new thought like a ray of light, that dispels the gloom. Often, He delights me with His promise of freedom from all bondage and limitation. That is my favourite. He whispers to my heart how much He would like to give to me, how much more there is; asking me patiently, when will you say yes, when will you receive it, it is all there, waiting for you.

Often enough I push Him away, though I know that He has all the answers, all that I so love and yearn for, all that I need; saying, as I would do with humans as well, I am busy, I must attend to this and to that; once I have dealt with all these other matters, I will be back to you. There is so incredibly much to attend to, I am forever late, no matter how early I get up.

He is there, patiently inviting me to let go and allow Him to comfort me. In my confused, obsessive state, His comfort seems not what I need, His love not as important as the hundred goals I have set myself. I want to admit how mistaken and blind I was!

When I have finally reached the point, once again, where I am on my knees and know I need Him and I want Him, that is when the glorious realisation dawns that His love is all that matters. That revolutionary thought is the point where my whole world is literally turned upside down.

And how He rejoices! Oh, my dearest God, I had no idea, how important I am to you, how you were longing for my love. I am taken aback to see that you want my love just as I was craving yours. I did not realise how much my love means to you, how you have been waiting for it - for me. I did not understand that someone as big and mighty as you could so much want the love of someone like me! You who created the universe, you the greatest power in the whole world, are desiring to be closely linked with me.

Suddenly I do not feel unloving or unlovable anymore. Suddenly I am smiling again, my eyes fill with tears, I am touched, I am sorry for keeping you waiting so long, I am eager to make it up to you. I am so happy, ready to abandon myself into the present moment of being as close and loving to you as I possibly can. What an honour to mean so much to you. What joy to have this intimacy with you. You are entirely mine, and I am yours. I will not let you down again. You are my priority, my heart's delight.

Now I understand why I do not need to look to others to make me feel loved and fulfilled. I see now why I can graciously relieve them of the burden of being responsible for how I feel about myself. I have the love of God that is shed abroad in my heart. It is almost like a physical sensation. Oh Lord, I did not realise it is true that you are so in love with me, that you think the world of me, thrilled, delighted with me. Here you stand, twenty-four seven, offering me your love with a warm smile. Inviting me to join you in a love relationship that will sweep me off my feet. Do I dare? Oh yes! My sweet Lord.

What is more, you show me that you value my heart. I cannot tell you how much it means to me that you think my love is sweet. That you see me as a loving person whose sweet love you want. Oh Lord, how gladly. How sorry I am for withholding it, for being too blind to see the part you want me to fill in our two-way relationship. I am here now, my love, here at last.

And suddenly it seems to me that the same softness and love and tenderness with which I relate to you, is in my eyes as I look at the birch trees around me! As if they too, long to be looked at with the love you have put in my heart, they too longing for my gentleness, just like you did. And looking at each tree with the eyes of one who is conscious that she is beloved of God Himself, it is like a ray of your love flows through me to them.

A wonderful verse

Trust steadily in God … (1 Corinthians 13:13 MSG)

As I went for my walk under blue skies and radiant morning sunshine, I pondered what this means for me.

Having faith in God and trusting Him on a continuous basis is something I need to practice. It is like strengthening a muscle, the faith-muscle, and it will only get stronger by repeatedly using it, just like I work on strengthening my body's muscles by exercising them most days on purpose. Yes, I do want to do that, I long to be more often aware when I am in faith and when I am not.

I want to practice noticing the connection between my thoughts and my moods and be ready to promptly turn situations and worries and things I am fearful about over to Him, trusting that He will take care of all that concerns me. I am longing to be steady in this alertness concerning my thought-life.

This morning I remembered I do have the choice of redirecting my thinking from heaviness and gloom back to His Word, trusting that it does what it says; enjoying the relief of casting my burdens onto Him who loves me. I am free to do that, it is all part of trusting, and there is no reason to delay doing it.

Trusting steadily in God, to me, also means acknowledging that He is here with me, that I am not alone, that He is very present indeed, with me, and in me. He rejoices every time I make a conscious connection with Him; I could make a point of telling Him I am doing what I am doing at that moment for Him. It is amazing to realize that any ordinary activity, no matter at all what it is, could become a joy, something beautiful, done thoughtfully and caringly and to the very best of my ability, because I do it unto the Lord.

I noticed, too, how my awareness of His presence and His appreciation for what I do, enables me to be more fully in the present moment; and this in turn leads me to gratitude. Gratitude itself is one of the loveliest states of being. Being thus grateful in the present moment is also a way for me to receive the peace with which He wants to comfort me. For how else can I receive His peace except in the present moment?

Practicing His presence in this way, trusting that He is truly here with me as I go about my business - I have discovered that it is equally the antidote to loneliness. And when I slip into a consciousness of isolation and forsakenness it is nothing more than a lapse in my commitment to live my life for Him. That is why this scripture says to do it *steadily*. I feel at this point in my life that I am more than ready and longing to master this discipline and commitment, and the way ahead looks inviting and hopeful.

The incorruptible life of God I

It is the spirit that gives life. The flesh profits nothing. The Words you speak to me, they are spirit, and they are life (John 6:63)

I have in my spirit the incorruptible life of God. What is more, I am not a body, I am spirit, because I have my Father's nature, and He is a spirit being. The beautiful verse above tells me that as I meditate on the scriptures and make God's Word my own, I am "taking in" food for my spirit. Not just any food, this food is pure life - life itself. How can regular daily doses of the Word that is life-giving spirit, not also effect my physical body?

It is already known that our thoughts, certain thought patterns, that we repeat on a daily basis, over and over again, will have an effect on our organic and physical health; and how through changing our mindset we might overcome a physical ailment.

If our ordinary mind has the power to influence our body, how much more powerful must be the results of thoughts that are inspired by God. His thoughts may be not quite comprehensible to our ordinary brains, but they are going to be all the more meaningful to our spirit! We find our spirit recognizing and lapping up the pure life that is contained in God's Word.

Imagine now the cells of your body. Instead of hearing the daily repetition of negative limiting thoughts they have heard for decades, and which are slowly but surely taking their toll on your organs and bodily systems – increasingly, they begin to hear a new song, a different tune. Imagine directing these divine truths directly at the cells of your body. You will be able to almost feel your cells' joy and delight at being fortified and restored with the stuff of life itself.

There is no reason that there should be any area of our physical existence that is out of reach of the new life of righteousness that we received when we received Jesus into our hearts. The Bible says that "He who has the Son has Life" (see 1 John 5:12). This new life is in our spirit. It cannot be taken from us; it cannot be lost. It is incorruptible, which means, it will never be affected by any outside circumstance or adversity, it is not subject to the wear and tear of time. It will always be perfect, glorious and brand-new, no matter what age we are.

It is therefore not going too far, to take what God says about me, utterly literal. I personally have found it incredibly emboldening and strengthening to declare that "this new life is in every cell of my blood, every bone of my body, every fibre of my being".

Let me attempt to describe what happens when I meditate along those lines: I try to imagine all the cells of my blood, each one of them having a smile on them, I seem to feel their joy at being alive, continuously moving through my body and bringing the powerful life of God to every nook and cranny. Through my many big and tiny blood vessels this life reaches to my littlest toe as well as to big organs like my heart or liver. It is forever flowing and bringing the good news of life to all members of my body. It seems to bring a blessing, cleansing and healing, and – this is no exaggeration - a mood of celebration and victory! Why indeed not?

However, this is not all. The life of God is in every bone of my body. I start picturing my bones, the massive, long ones in my thighs, the big joints at their ends, the tiny little bones in my fingers and feet. And the bone marrow, alive in their centre, producing more blood cells. I do not really know how the blood cells get from there into the bloodstream. What I do know though, is my new appreciation and joy about even my bones, which used to be the least of my considerations.

To me, it is like they are saying, yes, we are in it too, we too commit to contributing to this body. We too witness to the new life, we are brim-full of it, we do our part for the health and vitality of this body, we support the whole. You, other organs and blood, can count on us. We bones love the new life. We too are brand-new, there is no wear and tear, don't you worry.

Finally, there is every fibre of my being. Here I imagine absolutely all the material that my body is made of. My muscles, sinews, ligaments, cartilage, nerves, glands, my brain, my eyeballs, my teeth, my gums, my reproductive and digestive organs; and here in particular my gallbladder and pancreas, as they have always been my areas of concern.

It may sound strange, but can you imagine an organ having a victim mentality? Well, I believe this is what these two were suffering from before they too, were touched by the new life of God. It is like even these organs are beginning to say yes and to identify with who they are in Christ. It is literally as though they are agreeing that they have been helpless, weak and sorry for themselves for long enough now. It is like they are now claiming their position and power, saying, yes, we too are contributing to the whole.

We are supported by you all, and we in turn support you. Instead of gradually decaying and dying we protect the wellbeing of this body. We sing along with every other cell in this body, the new tune of salvation.

Like a tree

And he shall be like a tree planted by the rivers of water,
that bringeth forth his fruit in his season; his leaf also
shall not wither; and whatsoever he doeth shall prosper
(Psalm 1:3)

I am walking along the river. I am not sure I
should be doing that, on my own, because I am
not feeling well. I have been in hospital due to a
mysterious fainting spell, and I still feel strangely
lightheaded, not at all sure about my physical
strength. What if I collapse here, in a park, with
nobody around who knows me? Maybe I am a bit
irresponsible going for a walk without someone
accompanying me. My way of taking
responsibility is by focusing my mind on the
truth.

I am born of the Word. That is my nature.
Therefore, I am above sickness and disease, I am
infinitely superior to earthly conditions and
circumstances. I have the same spirit-nature as my
Father, I am not this physical body, I am spirit. So
therefore, I cannot be sick. Being born of the Word
means I have power, I am here for a reason, with

a purpose. There is no way I can be defeated by a physical condition. My spirit-nature makes me untouchable by sickness.

Where there is spirit there is life, and where there is life there cannot be death, or death processes like illness. It is either the one or the other. It is like light and darkness, they cannot be in the same place, they are mutually exclusive. I keep walking, never mind my wobbly legs.

I am also like a tree planted by the rivers of water. Does that contradict being born of the Word? No, it goes together very well. Once I am aware of my origins, of my spirit-nature, I need not fear where I am planted, I know I have been planted lovingly.

Regardless of where I came from, what my physical circumstances were, what my past was like, in truth I grew up graciously, lovely, like a young tree full of life; and as a mature tree I have strength and power, because I am deeply rooted where I was planted. There is no mistake about the place I am in, it is not a tragic error, a hopeless situation in which I am trapped, not at all.

I have learned to draw from the rivers of water. This living water is just like my true nature, which is born of the Word. It flows upwards in the tree and cools it; it nourishes the spirit-nature in me. It is exactly what I need to reaffirm my sovereignty, my superiority over any earthly condition, my dominion; and I am learning that I must draw that water, I must stretch my roots all the way to that river. If I do not, the tree will die; and so, I boldly do what a tree does.

I take what I need, for else the tree will rot, or go brittle and dry, and there will be no fruit. I do not want to die without having born fruit. It is a lie to think it is not worth the effort to dig in the roots until they reach the water, or that it is pointless. That is so not true. It is a lie also to think I cannot reach it, it is for others, not for me; a lie that I must wait till somebody else comes and brings me the water, fearful that I might be forgotten or might not receive as much as I need. I can and I will reach it myself.

Nor is it impertinent to avail myself of this life-giving water. I need not ask permission. When I was planted there, it was with this water source in mind. I thought I was planted in the wrong place;

I did not want to be here at all. I thought I was imprisoned and deprived by having to grow here, and that I would always remain a frail plant. I learn that there is nothing wrong with taking care of myself by taking advantage of my blessings.

Finally, how can a tree, inhabited by one who is born of the Word and watered by the Spirit not bear fruit? How can it go sick and die? There is no way it can fail, no way its' harvest will not be abundant and fragrant and beautiful, and no way this tree will ever be old or ugly.

And so, I arrive home from my walk by myself, not in an ambulance, but inspired and strengthened. Confident that I am and will be well, because it cannot be otherwise.

The incorruptible life of God II

The spirit of a man is the lamp of the Lord, searching all the inward parts of the belly (Proverbs 20:27)

I heard a pastor speak about the new life of righteousness, the incorruptible life of God in every cell of my blood, every bone of my body, every fibre of my being.

What a wonderful thing to see and feel the incorruptible life of God in every cell of my blood. My blood, warm and alive, flowing through my fabulous blood vessels to and from my heart that is joyously beating, pumping it throughout my body. Such richness, such aliveness. Thank you, dear blood. And yes, the life that you carry is incorruptible, pure, always one hundred percent potent and new. What an honour to be filled with this life and carry it everywhere.

The life in my bones: today I thought with gratitude about my bones, was amazed at their size and, length, acknowledging their presence in my body. Solid, strong, yet each one of them alive, living, and contributing to the whole. Can you imagine a sense of joy at realizing, these bones are real, they are part of me, they are magnificent? They are part of my wealth – all of these bones are mine, I am rich, because I have been blessed with these functioning, living, wonderful things. They stand, they withstand, I am proud of them.

Then there is the incorruptible life in every fibre of my being, and so also in every fibre of my belly. This may sound extreme, but I would say for most of my life my belly has been vacated. I was not there. Neither did I want to be there. I preferred being in my head.

I did not know how to take possession of my belly. Anything and anybody could come in there and take up residence. It was like the doors of my belly were always open to any intruder, whether they were good for me or not. I was soaking up anyone's vibes, anyone's "stuff" like a sponge.

However, I am no longer alone. Now my spirit is the candle of the Lord, searching the inmost parts of the belly! (see Proverbs 20:27) It is shining a light in all the dark corners on anything that does not belong there. Now I am back, now I claim ownership of my own belly. I have always known that my belly is also the place out of which flow rivers of living water (see John 7:38), and this is becoming real to me now. The rivers flow again. What had been literally dried out due to my absence is showing signs of life, in and around me.

Can you imagine the gladness of someone who has been exiled from their own territory for decades, and now they have come to take possession of it? As a conqueror, more than a conqueror even, (see Romans 8:31); because they are now bigger and more powerful than they were when they were first dispossessed, because they come filled with the incorruptible life of God.

I see my organs, that had been in a state of contraction all my life, taking up space now; daring to expand and be, to be present. They are fortified by the incorruptible life of Christ in my spirit. Resisting anything foreign that wants to come back, staring them in the eye and asserting my authority. "Resist the devil, and he will flee from you." (see James 4:7)

And while it is in the full knowledge that it is the greater One who lives in me that enables me to resist and give no space to the intruders, still at the same time I never had a more joyous consciousness of myself. This is me. How blessed I am with even just this body; how rich, how much reason to be excited! Me and my organs, my bones, my blood, a presence to be reckoned with, here to impact the world.

My Lover

I am my beloved's, and my beloved is mine. He feeds his flock among the lilies (Song of Solomon 6:3)

As I went for a walk one October afternoon, years ago, I intended to meditate on God's love for me. I knew spending an hour moving my body out in the fresh air and thinking about God's Word is the best thing I can do to escape my negativity.

I had learned from experience that God's love can in fact take my feelings of loneliness and abandonment away, fill the void. However, my mind was often circling around, even obsessing about, another person, and I was longing for this guy to make me happy, wanting to do almost anything for a little love and attention from him!

It is amazing how I can slip into this pattern every so often, forgetting that it is I who is responsible for my own happiness. I know so well that I must not make my joy and peace and self-worth dependent on someone else's attention.

While changing my mental habits seems to be a learning process that takes me a long time, I am happy to say that I am however making progress. I do have peaceful times where I understand and know that I am whole, complete, and loveable already, regardless of what my circumstances look like. Each time I forget, my heart lets me know that I am off-track.

That particular afternoon I asked God to talk to me, doing my best to summon and give Him my willingness to *understand* how much He loves me. I was willing to allow Him a chance to change my mind. I was sick of my own attitude and was longing to let myself be persuaded that God's love is worth taking seriously.

Over the course of my one-hour walk a multitude of thoughts then occurred to me which I had never had before, and it was indeed like He was describing His relationship to me in a way which completely surprised me.

He seemed to ask me, Do you not think I have the same qualities of masculinity and strength, perseverance and drive and success that you admire in this man? Do you not know I am the source of all fine qualities that a man can have?

You know in your heart that I too can make you

feel beautiful and desirable (quite apart from the fact that I have *made* you beautiful and desirable), that I am more than willing to take care of you and protect you, spoil you, charm you, make you laugh, hold you and comfort you. Do not forget that I own the world and all I have is yours and I have laid it at your feet. Do you really believe I have less to offer than your well-off man?

Can you believe that I truly think about you all the time, much more so than any human could ever do? However, do you realize that I appreciate your love and sweetness no less than a man could do?

I too rejoice and smile when you love and praise me, I too long for your company, your closeness, your attention, your appreciation, no less than any man you want to give your heart to. I know the love that is inside you, after all I have put it there. I know your tenderness and devotion, and they belong to me, first.

Like a man, I too like you to *see* all the tokens of my love, all that I am giving to you to make you happy, all that I put before you every day, that I did just for you.

Your childlike delight in fallen autumn leaves, I have put that emotion in you. Your ability to experience and enjoy the season of autumn, the impulse and longing to mark this season in some way, celebrate it, that's your creativity which I have put into you. And I invite you to enjoy the autumn, enjoy every day."

That particular autumn, I felt like, along with making me feel loved, He had unleashed a wave of freedom and playfulness in me. I am learning that enjoying the life He has given me is absolutely part of His will for me too, and even my ability to rejoice and delight myself are part of His gifts of love to me.

The joy of the Lord

The joy of the Lord is your strength (Nehemiah 8:10)

For ye shall go out with joy and be led forth with peace; the mountains and the hills shall break forth before you into singing, and all the trees of the field shall clap their hands (Isaiah 55:12)

The simple joy to be alive: it is in the ray of the evening sun lighting up a spot in the thicket between the young trees, making the highlighted plant in the undergrowth look as if it wants me to hear it sing of the sweetness that it is a part of, happy that I am noticing it. It is in the amazing play of light and shade on the path lying before me as I walk against the low evening sun causing every single stone sticking out of the ground, every little tuft of grass, to cast a shadow. I feel like I have never seen anything so spectacular, it is like I am being wowed from the moment I enter the little forest.

Later on, during the same walk, I am again directly walking into the sun which makes it fairly impossible to see anything; I am feeling intoxicated, like drunk with all that light; like being invited to let myself go and engage with the exuberance of it all. The joy is in seeing the long strip of green being lit up by the evening sun, again, spectacularly, richly, lavishly, feeling so like the beauty that is typical of an autumn evening; I have to turn to the sun and say thank you, oh thank you, what a treat.

I can feel the sunshine through the material of my black jeans, lovely and warm, like a caress. The sun peeping friendly through the branches of the trees, its rays glistening – I know I am loved, I know this is all for my benefit.

The joy of the Lord in the oak leaves of a young tree, those classical, elegant oakleaves, still green, looking so well, so abundant, the little oak tree and its neighbouring bigger tree doing splendidly. I want to thank them for being there. Elsewhere a little twig with bright yellow oak leaves on the ground, a beautiful shade of yellow that delights me with its purity, a shade that is in me too. Thank you my dear.

Some plant whose leaves are taking on varying shades of orange and red: I stand and give them my appreciation and it is as if they are delighted to be noticed and give me their own joy of the Lord. They sway ever so gently in the movement of the air around us; it is like they have been waiting for me all along. Some tall white grasses, reflecting the evening light, their contrast against the dark green foliage of brambles and shrubs remarkable; moving almost imperceptibly in the air.

They all know, they know perfectly well, the joy of the Lord, and they are so glad I came to share it with them for a few moments. Two young tree trunks, a matt sheen on their greyish green bark, growing closely, maybe from the same root, reminding me of two lovers, or siblings, as if growing up they are relating to each other, happy to be together. I am happy for them, for their youthfulness, vigour, beauty.

I find the joy of the Lord also in the abundant growth of the tall ferns, like every year, their feathery leaves mostly still green but some already turned into that cinnamon colour that I love, like every year. So ample, plentiful, elegant too. How I appreciate them. They are like a clan, a family apart, unlike anything else in the wood.

The little path leading off to the right, its gravel still so white and new looking, gently meandering between green growth on both sides, so sweet-looking, so content to be a path, to have me walk on it if I want or not to have me walk on it; in either case content, peaceful, happy to be what it is. I stand and love it. I listen to the silence, the beautiful stillness in the wood, the perfection of it all. Thank you, thank you.

The joy of the Lord in the two dogs coming towards me, red setters with beautiful rusty coloured hair, full of life, carefree, enthusiastic; and in the eleven-week-old boxer puppy. The joy in sharing a friendly greeting with other happy walkers, happy in each other's company, happy to say hello.

The community of nettles, on the side of the path, all the way back to the carpark, they are my friends. We know each other well. There was a time I used to harvest and eat them. These are small and a little thin, they probably will not grow much more before the winter. But I believe they do not mind. They are content to be nettles, still getting a chance to join in the song of nature before the year is up. They are here for me, I thank them, I know of their power, their unassuming reliability. Thank you, my dears.

Another scripture comes to mind, "For ye shall go out with joy, and be led forth with peace; the mountains and the hills shall break forth before you into singing, and all the trees of the field shall clap their hands. Isaiah 55:12 I love this. It is true, they do. And yes, this is me! That is why it is so good to go out; *intending* to find that joy and be grateful for it, allowing myself to be shown, respectfully asking for it, listening for that sweetness that all things in nature are so aware of, eager to show me. Inviting me to look through their eyes, to hear the trees clap their hands.

Welcoming me as if I am a guest of honour, as if I am holy like them. Like they need me to receive their gifts, and I need them to receive my appreciation, for in doing so and loving them back we complement each other.

This is my true strength because it is of the Lord. That means it is holy, it is eternal, I can never lose it, and it cannot be taken from me. I can have it always because it is *mine*; and it is not only pleasant and beautiful, gifting me with a happy time like today in the woods, it is my *strength*. Does that not mean, whenever I feel weak or powerless, I have forgotten about my beautiful strength?

It means there is no reason to ever again believe that permission to be joyful must be given by anyone or anything outside of me; or that my joy can only unfold and be felt if circumstances allow it. My strength is not actually in controlling things around me, because it is not there at all, it is simply in my joy. That feels a lot better.

We all know it is true. When I am truly joyful, I am so much stronger. Joy is soft and easy, it is irresistible, and even contagious. My joy is in the Lord, and my strength is in my joy. Thank you, thank you, thank you.

Me, the one with the sad eyes, haunted by depression – and yet its very opposite, joy, is my strength. Is it possible I should be a specialist in that which seemed to have eluded me most of my life? It seems the world is waiting for it.

My fruitful field

Until the spirit is poured upon us from on high, and the wilderness becomes a fruitful field, and the fruitful field is counted as a forest (Isaiah 32:15)

Every time I emerge victoriously from another "attack" of depression, it is because God has changed my mindset from darkness to light. In my joyous relief I often feel inspired to make a note of how it happened; I think it is important to remember how I got there so that I will become more and more conscious and adept at choosing God's thoughts about me. The other reason is so that others can see that asking Him for help really works!

I remember looking for help a few years ago, and a lady kindly suggested to me to say to myself, "The Lord is my shepherd, I shall not want" (Psalm 23:1). I thought to myself, I believe that this works for you, but I cannot see how it is going to help me. That is because at the time I had not yet understood that I need to meditate on a precious Word like that, I cannot figure it out with my rational brain but need to ask the Holy Spirit for a *revelation* of it. I need to be helped up to a higher level to be able to appreciate God's thoughts about me, and I need to engage my heart.

I have become conscious enough to realise that every morning as I open my eyes, I have an array of options of what I could focus my mind on. It is so worthwhile to start my day by turning to God's Word and devote some time to thinking about it and asking for an insight that will sustain me for the day. This morning I turned to Isaiah 32:15.

It says that God has turned my "wilderness" into a "fruitful field". It is easy to visualise the wilderness: the nettles, thistles, brambles and dock leaf of my negative thinking. At the very least they are a nuisance, making it hard to walk. Some of these weeds, such as resentment and unforgiveness have deep roots, so hard to remove; but most of these intruders are painful when you come in contact with them, scratchy when you fall into their thorns. Between them, they keep choking everything you have tried to plant, leaving very little space for anything beautiful.

What about the "fruitful field" then? I had

meditated on that scripture before, and it had spoken to me. I think what happened next, was due to my willingness to ask and be shown again. Because then I remembered: The fruitful field is right here; or rather, it is where I am. It is Heaven, the Kingdom; and from one instant to another I realised that is where I am.

I can only describe it as a softening and widening on the inside of me. It is a switch from being confined to my earthly perception of things to seeing with the eyes of the Spirit. And with it comes the instant realisation that I am abundant and blessed beyond words. There is such affluence in my fruitful field that I want to laugh at the idea of scarcity.

All of a sudden, I have the certain awareness of my wealth, the vastness of what has been entrusted to me, and with it my own capacity to embrace it all and take care of it with ease. There is no effort or struggle in being in charge of all this; there is lightness, joy, and happy laughter. I have so much more than I need - plenty enough to give it away, for the supply is unlimited, no end to what I can pass on, and no greater joy than doing just that.

And as I now look around me, in my kitchen, my sitting-room, my garden, everything simply confirms what I have seen in the Spirit. All the things that are good and beautiful around me are a reflection of the fruitfulness of my field. They are countless examples of the riches that my spirit is beginning to grasp. Lots of little manifestations of the truth; but really, they are just the icing on the cake, and they are just the beginning.

The important thing is that they are not the source of my joy. I am no longer crawling on the ground trying to pull myself up. Instead, I have risen above my earthly circumstances, like an eagle, because I have understood that my life is way more, way vaster than the limited existence that I used to believe in. Viewed from up here, the thought of the afflicted girl struggling to find joy in life, is just meaningless.

I open the door of my fridge, and I see the goodness of God in all the vegetables in there. They too grew in my fruitful field. Can you imagine feeling love for the beauty of a celeriac?

Well, I did. The tulips in the garden, in radiant, cheerful colours, all speak of the joy of God. Everything agrees, "all creation" reaffirms that yes, God is great. It is His pleasure and His will to give me His Kingdom, and His will is now.

My inheritance

The lines have fallen to me in pleasant places; Yes, I have a good inheritance (Psalm 16:6)

I have heard it mentioned many times, that my Father in Heaven wants me to receive his blessings now, in this life, not only when I am no longer walking this earth. At least in theory I understand that He does not want me to suffer through my life in scarcity and want. There are plenty of scriptures confirming this.

If God's Word says I am blessed, and that His blessing makes one rich and He adds no sorrow with it (see Proverbs 10:22), then it must be so and I would not argue with that; but somehow my belief was, I must wait till *one day* I will claim those blessings. Maybe when I have "made it" in this world, when I have finally discovered how and where I fit in and belong, when I have established myself. *Then* I can spend whatever time is left looking at the inheritance which is not of this world and enjoying my Father's blessings.

It took me until now to realize that maybe I was trying to put the cart before the horse. Matthew 6:33 says, we should first seek the Kingdom of God and His righteousness, and all these things will be added to us. I used to think I did value the Kingdom of God first and foremost; but really, I was always trying to compromise. Could I really dare going for what I dearly want to do, turn my back on the system of the world and trust that God's laws will work for me?

During years of inner conflict and tension I was confused, yet in my spirit I knew all along what I wanted, and I am passionate about it. It is the only thing that will satisfy me.

Parallel to my efforts and struggling in the world, my spirit has been expanding, and the vistas that I saw only vaguely to begin with, seem to increase and become more tangible and more real almost daily. What my spirit is showing me, and the urge to share my delight about it by for instance writing it down, the prompting to go ahead and *do it*, the thought that it might be worthwhile sharing has grown into a conviction.

"The lines" mentioned in Psalm 16 are the

outlines of the land that has been allotted to me. It is the section of life, the particular circumstances that have been apportioned to me. It talks about "pleasant places", and later in the same psalm it says, "in your presence is fullness of joy and pleasures forever more". Well, if that is so, then I must have been looking in the wrong place, when all I saw was turmoil. If this is my inheritance, then let me find it. I am ready for it now.

You may see the surface of the land you have inherited, the good points and the not so good ones. I have looked around at the land of others and found my lot to be unfair; have tried to make the best of it. At the same time, I resigned myself to admitting I had not done anything much with it. I spent many years staring at my land, feeling sorry for myself, wondering, is this all there is? I was never guessing that there were untold treasures hidden in the depths of it.

Sometimes you have to dig. It is true that gold, oil, will not come up by themselves. As far as I know you have to mine it, it requires some effort and patience. I am no longer afraid to look deeper. If God says my inheritance is in there, then I will apply all I have learned to claim it. I will show it to you, and the more of it I show to you, the more I will find. It will bring me such joy, because finally I am doing something for you. I am blessed to be able to delight myself in what is revealed to my spirit, and I am blessed if I manage to put that delight into words and pass it on to others. It seems like this inheritance is at the same time my purpose.

My portion

O Lord, You are the portion of my inheritance and my cup; You maintain my lot (Psalm 16:5)

When a thought finally gains the upper hand in my mind and allows me to snap out of a heavy, dark mood back into the sunshine, to me, this a miracle. This time it happens as I remember a line from one of my favourite worship songs "You're my portion..." It is like a ray of light clearing away cobwebs and clutter, instilling energy into me. Like a wilting flower, my head, which has been literally hanging with tiredness till my chin nearly touched my chest, lifts up again. My eyes which kept drooping suddenly open wide. I am awake! There is a ray of hope here, something to hold on to.

Suddenly I find my willingness to have a fresh look at God's Word, to give it a chance. Instead of saying "no" to everything, I am now ready for the answer. I am willing to hear now. My ears are no longer blocked with negativity. For "faith comes by hearing, and hearing by the Word of God" (see Romans 10:17). God being my portion means I have everything I need, and all the answers to every situation as well. The remembrance that I have it all is chasing away the heaviness!

Now I am willing to study, to find out once again what the Word says. It is true that in order to find my treasure and heritage, I must look there. I recognize that in the course of the last days, I had slipped back into looking for solutions and trying to have everything under control *in my own strength.* I kept looking for satisfaction in what I could see in my physical world and in thoughts and plans I thought with my physical brain. No wonder I got bogged down in frustration and uncertainty, seeing no life, no colour, no excitement.

It was not until today that I remembered I always must look on the inside first, before I can see the beauty and riches outside. It just will not work the other way round. I was willing to step back and be shown, turn to the Word and give it first place again.

The scripture I was looking at was Acts 20:32: *And now, brethren, I commend you to God, and to the word of his grace, which is able to build you up and give you an inheritance among all them which are sanctified.*

I am not a helpless candle in the wind anymore, because I am being built up. That is exactly what I need. "Strengthened in my inner man" which is like a giant when it rises inside me; through the power of God's Spirit which is in His Word. On top of that, I am given an inheritance! I have been shown how to access that inheritance, I have the key. I can feel the refreshing new willingness to appropriate all the promises of the Word into my life.

I also recognise, it is not by trying to scrape together all I can see around me and assembling it into an abundant life; trying to squeeze joy and gratitude out of what this world has to offer. The beauty and abundance I see around me are first and foremost inside me. They are of course a reflection of the glory of what the Holy Spirit can show me in the Word.

What lifts my depression is the recognition, that I cannot be deprived or disadvantaged in my life if I have all my inheritance already inside me!

In addition, I found another lovely element to

add to the joy about my portion and inheritance. In Philemon 1:6 I am asked to acknowledge all the good that is in me in Christ Jesus, and right now, this is becoming easier again. Not only does it result in me feeling happier once more, but I am also being promised that it will increase "the effectiveness of the sharing of my faith". This is again, exactly what I need to hear, because when I feel unworthy and miserable, of course I doubt my ability and calling to share and reach anyone else with my faith.

This makes perfect sense to me. I believe, having the boldness of acknowledging the good that is in me is the greatest and most convincing teaching aid for me and for anyone who longs to uplift others. My mind understands and can explain all this; now let me demonstrate the genuine joy that goes with it and that is the proof and the attractive power of what I am talking about.

Have and enjoy

The thief comes only in order to steal and kill and destroy. I have come that they may have and enjoy life, and have it in abundance (to the full, till it overflows). (John 10:10 AMP)

If Jesus came that we might have and enjoy life more abundantly, and the original word in the Bible for "have" can also be translated as "enjoy", then there must be a connection between the two, between having and enjoying something.

Could it be then that we only truly "have" something once we enjoy it? Does it then not also follow that if I want to learn that God is with me, and I *have* Him in my life, on the inside of me, then I must make the effort to enjoy Him? It is only by enjoying His presence that I really have it. Oh, I am willing to learn that!

By giving Him my joy, my relationship with Him is kept alive and growing ever more real. Let me remember this! I realise it is I who needs to be the one to consciously water and nurture that joy.

This is interesting. We normally think the other way round. We say, I cannot enjoy something until I am sure I have it. First, I must have it, ideally own it, then I can enjoy it. Yet if have and enjoy essentially mean the same thing, then maybe my emphasis should be on developing my ability to enjoy, rather than on scheming for ways to have the object of my desire.

So much is given freely, yet a gift needs to be received to be a gift. How do I receive the gift of life if not by enjoying it, valuing, appreciating it? Quite possibly, what we do not enjoy we might lose. Not only might it literally disappear out of our life, but it is anyway lost to us if we do not appreciate it. So, you might add gratitude to the having and enjoying.

In order to "have and enjoy" the abundant life that Jesus came, suffered and died for us to have, I must make sure to keep alive the joy and appreciation for all the aspects of the life I have been given.

If the Bible says He gave us richly all things to enjoy (see 1 Timothy 6:17), then that means I am rich, and all things are mine. Gosh, what a profound statement! Now we are invited to dare walking in the hugeness of this truth! Then, in order to grasp the measure of riches I have been given, I must do my part, and enjoy them. In order to receive all things, I need to open my heart, let them in and keep enjoying them. That is my job.

It looks like it is only by getting big enough and our hearts wide enough to embrace and enjoy all that we wish for, that we can "have" it. What God is looking for in order to bless us, is therefore not suffering and hardship, but our readiness to enjoy His gifts. We do not make Him smile as we struggle in the effort to obtain and deserve a good thing in our life; because a gift cannot be earned, only received, thankfully and joyously.

Far away in Australia

Now faith is the substance of things hoped for, the evidence of things not seen (Hebrews 11:1)

Recently I found myself depressed and worried about the latest developments in my eldest daughter's life. Together with her partner and their two young children they left Ireland and went to Australia some five years ago. While there had been troubled times due to his heavy drinking over the years even before they left, he now has developed a serious addiction to crystal meth. Picturing the heartache and problems for all involved, left me feeling helpless and like a dark cloud was hanging over me for a couple of days. Until I realised, I can pray and I can believe.

I have been meditating on the love of God, and I can see and believe my daughter's mind and body flooded with it and all that strain flushed out. This love relieves her mind of the heaviness that has been burdening it and frees her body of the tension and tiredness resulting from years of conflict and arguing. Her fears and worries are falling off her, and the relief she experiences in every fibre and every organ of her body is so profound that I can almost feel it in my own, as I think of her.

She is enveloped and comforted by that love, and she sheds a tear of gratitude as she snuggles into the warm and safe arms of Love. Feeling surrounded and held and shielded, her heart that had been aching is made whole and beats with the joy and enthusiasm that were hers as a child. Certain of the presence within her, she can stand tall now, holding her head up high, she feels light and free, and she cannot help but love back the Love that loved her first (see 1 John 4:19).

Suddenly she is proud of who she is and feels a joyful optimism in the knowledge that she can face anything because she is not alone in this. A power greater than herself is at her side waiting for her to turn all the things over to Him; things that have been too much for so long and over which she is powerless.

It is a voice that reminds her that she is lovely, and she is worth it, reminds her of all her talents and remarkable assets, resourcefulness and intelligence. The voice gradually teaches her about compassion and detachment with love, of letting go and having faith. She is learning that she is officially allowed to enjoy her life and live one day at a time.

She is shown that she does not have to solve this entire situation but that she can step off the merry-go-round of arguing and fighting, conflict and insanity. And thus, I see her exuding adult confidence and authority and smiling reassuringly at her children, the man she has started a new relationship with, and even at her former partner, leaving them free and allowing them each to go through their own experiences and learn and grow from them.

I see them as five people who each in their own way have been struggling to keep going despite their broken hearts. Fragile hearts which in my opinion can be healed only by a love that is not of this world. And every time the heavy clouds threaten to darken my own mind as I think of them, I choose strength instead of fear. I see each one of them in turn injected with a dose of that love which alone can take the pain away.

I see my granddaughter and grandson forgiving their parents, their hearts shielded and protected from darkness and bitterness. They are getting strong as they grow up, free from worry, fear, or co-dependency. I see them given another shot at a carefree childhood, I see grace protecting them from too much responsibility and from being burdened too early with adult problems.

Grace performing the miracle of keeping their sanity intact, and soothing and repairing whatever has been affected. I see them smiling openly and with relief and with the childlike innocence to which they are entitled.

I see the adults in this scenario, my daughter and her former partner and her current partner, forgiving each other and themselves, see them extending compassion to one another. I see them leaning without reserve on that Love that is always ready to comfort and take the pain away. I see them again and again going there to receive the encouragement and praise and support and gentleness they crave and that they did not know where to find. I see them, for the first time, feeling joy in who they are, confidence that they can face the world, even without drugs, without addiction of any kind.

They are adults who trust in their strength and maturity and have faith that they are helped to do what they could not do of themselves. I see them smiling at each other and smiling at their reflection in the mirror.

Like me, they are learning to say no to the lies of a destructive mindset, learning that instead, they can choose to think and see the positive that they really want. And thinking of them, I do not actually feel far away, depressed and powerless in the face of their problems, but I feel close to them, and I do in fact feel happy for them. As if all that I have seen in my mind's eye has already come to pass.

The illusion of loneliness

And it shall come to pass in that day, that his burden shall be taken away from off your shoulder, and his yoke from off your neck, and the yoke shall be destroyed because of the anointing (Isaiah 10:27)

My devotional today is talking about how the burden has been taken off my shoulders and the devil's yoke off my neck; and not only that, but it has also been destroyed because of the anointing. The anointing means the Holy Spirit has been poured upon me. I have that anointing, I have received it, and the Bible also says that it will abide in me forever. That means I have it right now, even if I do not always feel it. Let that anointing deal with the yoke of negative thinking. Speak to me about the illusion of loneliness!

Yes, loneliness truly is an illusion, Carla. It is not a fact, it is consciousness, a way of looking at life, a way of interpreting circumstances, but it is only there if you believe it is. Is it not just a certain sequence of thoughts that leads to a certain familiar bleakness? There is no power attached to certain times of the day, certain days of the week, certain times of the year, to make you miserable and bring up the feeling of isolation.

The many times when you found relief in meditating on the Scriptures, or on your devotional reading, what happened to your sense of loneliness? Sometimes it led to not only relief but real joy, a definite renewal of your mind, new excitement about life.

You were reminded of who you are in Christ, who you are in truth, and what you have as a child of God. The one most powerful message for you has been for a while now, that as a child of God who walks in love, you cannot be disadvantaged. Wow. Everything has already been freely given to you, the world is yours, you have it all.

You are told that you need to claim it and speak it into existence. You will get the hang of it. You have God's Word at work in you, and you are learning daily, how to use it and put it into practice. How can you be a helpless victim of loneliness then? Suddenly the whole idea of it has vanished, as if it was literally nothing but a misperception of yourself, a delusion, that's all.

Is it not remarkable that nothing in your circumstances has changed, all that needed to change was your attitude, your mind. Suddenly your mindset is one of expectation and excitement, you are looking out and forward. Suddenly you see nothing but possibilities. You are joyous anyway, no matter what happens next. You would not dream of seeing yourself as lonely – instead, you consider yourself fortunate and privileged and very blessed. Willing and ready to follow God's personal message to you, See what you have! Behold, look!

Is that not the ultimate proof that loneliness is an illusion, a lie? Just look how far you have come already, how far God has already brought you out of isolation; how much more you are able to enjoy by yourself, and also when you go "out there".

You will get bolder in claiming the relationships and friendships you want. You have come this far, why would God not also bring you further, all the way?

So much to give

It is true, there is another Carla, who has long outgrown and left behind the broken person I used to be that prefers to isolate herself and push others away in order to stay safe. This other me is not helpless anymore. "For God has not given us a spirit of fear, but a spirit of power and love, and a sound mind" (see 2 Timothy 1:7). Whenever I slip back into self-condemnation, let me ask, is this scripture the truth about me or is it not, do I believe God's Word or do I not? I know in my heart it is true. Help me to believe it and act on it.

At least, something in me is willing to pursue that line of thought; and I find plenty more evidence in God's Word that I am not the unloving person my darkest thoughts make me out to be. Like an advocate in my defence the Holy Spirit reminds me that "the love of God has been shed abroad in my heart by the Holy Spirit" (see Romans 5:5).

I know this love, the memory of it is almost like a sensation in my belly. And once again, *by grace,* I remember that I like this Carla. There is nothing wrong with her. She has so much to give, and she gives out of the abundance inside of her, with a smile, happily, regardless of what anyone's reaction will be. This Carla is much bigger, wider and stronger than my old self.

All of a sudden, reaching out and making contact is not difficult, suddenly the communication is all there, it is not complicated. I manage to resist the attraction of the old fear. Being loving, being giving, is a little like walking freely, without holding on to anything else, without the safety net of my old negative thinking. The plan B of retreating in self-defence is now not an option.

I stay open, I stay giving, I stay present. It is chancing to be free, risking having no agenda, no preconceived ideas, just stepping out in faith. The person I interact with is off the hook, they are allowed to be where they are and who they are. We relate in freedom, two whole complete individuals, connecting for a while. I do not pull, I do not grasp, I do not obsess. I have once again defeated the urge to isolate myself and to shut others out of my life, I have won a victory!

A lamp unto my feet

Your Word is a lamp unto my feet and a light unto my path (Psalm 119:105)

I keep longing to know what God's will for me is, what He would have me do, especially when it comes to making big decisions concerning my future that will also have an impact on others.

How could the guidance I need be contained in God's Word?

Let me first of all acknowledge, if I am offered a lamp through God's Word, as the above verse says, then there must be a need for one. That means without this source of light I am in the dark. I will not argue with that; that is how I tend to feel when faced with the need to make a decision.

Imagine being in the dark. This morning as I was waiting in my car at the traffic lights in town, I saw a blind man finding his way along the footpath with the help of his white stick. He was touching the metal fence near the place where the pedestrians cross, slowly moving along it until his stick told him this is the place where the barrier ends and where you can cross over.

If you cannot see where you are going you are forced to put a lot of attention into avoiding danger and not hurting yourself. Besides, your progress would be slow. Could it be God was showing me this morning that this is how I move through my life whenever I try to do it without His Word?

Mind you, it is a lamp unto my *feet!* I remember another place where Scripture tells us about God's concern for our feet, where we are carried by angels, so we do not dash our foot against a stone (see Psalm 91:12). It hurts to knock your toes against an unexpected obstacle!

I like dreaming and imagining the bigger picture, God's big plan for me, such as becoming someone who through her own life witnesses to what it is like to live in the joy of the Lord. I love the idea of reflecting in my own life the glory of the Kingdom of Heaven, even while still on this earth. However, in order to get there, I need to use these feet I have been given. I need to set one foot before the other. If I want to run the race set before me (see Hebrews 12:1-2), I need to begin by taking steps.

I used to have a recurrent dream of running and not being able to move forward, a nightmare of being stuck. Whereas I have not had that dream in a very long time, the feeling of being "stuck" in certain areas of my life is still an issue. I know, one reason for my inability to move forward is fear; and is it not natural to be scared when you grope in the dark trying to find a spot safe enough to set your foot on?

So now I have a lamp showing me where to put my feet. Being able to see clearly helps to identify what you are actually looking at. What may have seemed good enough in the half-light or even fool-proof in the dark could be recognized as cracked and even hazardous. That is a great help.

Then again, you might discover a place solid enough to trust, a place that can hold your weight as you venture forward; and you would never have looked there because you did not think there was anything there for you, or because that place just did not look like what you had in mind for yourself. Yet in the light of the lamp, you recognize that it is perfect.

You might recognise with a gasp that it was in fact made especially for you. And though you may be not quite sure what the next step after that will be you trust that this is right.

I believe, the lamp is the joy and the strength that energizes me when my spirit has been "lit up" so to speak, by meditating on God's Word. I am discovering for myself, and I am in the process of learning, that what I need to do, is hold that light up as I take a step in my life. If the light remains bright, the joy stays, the life in me is still strong, then my action must be in line with the Word. And if it is not, then before long, it will be.

The Word says so much about *me,* about who I am, what I have and what I can do in Christ. Therefore, it stands to reason that taking in and internalizing what I am shown in it will be a guideline by which to assess whether what I am doing is in line with and progressing me towards God's goal for me or not.

I am grateful that I have been given a lamp helping me to take steps and learning to trust that it is possible to make decisions and find my way by its light; and that keeping that light alive is what I need to do in order to be able to continue moving forward. While it is so tempting to try and force a way forward in the darkness of my own limited vision, I learn to trust that God's way is ultimately a lot more likely to succeed.

The image of God's Word as a light unto my *path* gives me joy. There are so many paths to choose from. How am I supposed to know which is for me? I look for the one that has been lit up for me. If it is for me, I will perceive the light, the path will invite me, and I will be drawn to it. My delight in the brightness along the way is the same delight I feel about God's Word. And I become less obsessed with reaching the goal, and way more involved with the journey itself.

It would not make sense to think that God would put me into this world without guiding me in the way that I should go, without giving me a means by which to check in with Him and find out if I am on the right track. Nor would it make sense that I should be the one who has been denied access to His will for me. His means of communication with me is the Holy Spirit speaking to my spirit.

There are so many decisions and choices to be made daily, not only the big life-changing ones, but it goes all the way to helping me decide what to wear today, whether to buy this product or that, whether to drive a different way to work today. I have heard it said that the Holy Spirit is interested in *all* these things, everything concerning me, every day, every minute of my life. That is amazing!

Recently I heard a woman tell a story where on a busy motorway the car in front of the one she and her adult children were traveling in, was breaking suddenly, forcing them to do likewise. The car behind them, though, did not come to a halt until it had collided with the back of theirs. Only seconds before that, her daughter had realized she was not wearing her seatbelt and put it on. The woman said, if she had done that a few seconds later, her daughter would have crashed through the windscreen.

I do believe that keeping our minds focused on God's Word, turning it over in our thoughts pretty much all day long, instead of following our ordinary everyday thoughts for too long, will have a benefit we cannot even imagine. It puts us in a mindset of listening, ensures that we have an "open mind", a softer attitude in general. To me, that is "the light unto my path".

I believe it is in that frame of mind that you are more likely to hear the nudging of the Holy Spirit, the small voice that suggests putting your seatbelt on, RIGHT NOW. And as you exceptionally buy your jam in the health food store where you do not normally go, you get talking with someone who turns out to be the piano teacher you had been looking for who is just the right person for your child and for your budget.

Gloriously riding on

Therefore, if any man be in Christ, he is a new creature: old things are passed away; behold, all things are become new (2 Corinthians 5:17)

There is nothing in the world to stop me from using my mind in a beneficial way. There is nothing to prevent me from meditating on God's Word or Word-based ideas and taking them very personal and literally; nothing to limit the depth and meaning with which I invest these thoughts. Above all, the insight and liberty I gain during these meditations, the truths they contain, are not limited to my times of reflection. They can remain my reality and consciousness and need not be one fraction less valid, when I go about my everyday business.

In a devotional, years ago, I came across a line which fascinated me; and though I have never in my life sat on an actual horse, there is part of me that knows what this is talking about:

I am gloriously riding on with the Lord in the realms of glory, where I prosper, and all my needs are met.

It is the consciousness where I know how

privileged I am and perceive the newness and freshness of every moment. It is always there, waiting for me to choose it, a promise of unlimited possibilities that delights me, and adds radiance to my life. It is an excitement that cannot be explained, like the joy with which a toddler might greet the new day; a loveliness that does not grow old or stale, because it is forever young. To live and move in this consciousness is what I consider glorious.

I am riding on, not stagnant, nor trapped. I am moving. I am not dragging my feet, nor crawling. I am realizing that riding on with the Lord, following Him, does not mean perpetually struggling. It is a mode of travelling which is far superior to the earthbound slow progress I would make by relying on myself alone. Instead, I am invited to progress and expand into Him. If another translation for glory is wholeness or fullness, then it is all about having the boldness to trust in His wholeness, knowing that the joy of beholding His glory includes the joy about my own completeness.

Of myself, I could never find these realms of glory, would not know where to look, and even if

I looked straight at them, I would not recognize them. But as a new creation in Christ Jesus, I begin to understand that the realms of glory are within me. Jesus knows His way around here, He knows what He is talking about, He knows how to walk here, guides and teaches me how to conduct myself. He knows how to live and move naturally as a child of the Most High, knows all that belongs to me in the Kingdom of God, and also what is expected of me here. He will bring me all the way, step by step, patiently, until I understand where I am and who I am in His Kingdom.

Here I prosper, and all my needs are already met, because it is not my Father's will that I should want for anything (see Psalm 23:1). Lack does not exist in His Kingdom. He delights in the prosperity of His children (see Psalm 35:27), and His giving is not subject to the world's rules or approval. He does not need to ask the world's permission to love and bless and take care of His children.

I am not leading two lives, one in the spirit and one in this world, and I am not two persons, one who lives in the presence of God, unlimited as a child and citizen of Heaven, and the other suffering under the conditions of my earthly existence. There is no situation where I have fallen out of His favour, where I am suddenly excluded from His Kingdom. I still dwell in the secret place of the Most High (see Psalm 91). The realms of glory extend all the way to my everyday life in my hometown because *I* am there. As the Kingdom and the glory remain inside me, I cannot be stripped of them. I remain under no laws but God's, and no earthly laws can override them.

Thank you, God, for giving me a strong and unlimited mind and consciousness.

God's beauty

He has made everything beautiful in its time (Ecclesiastes 3:11)

"My whole life is an epitome of God's beauty" - I found these beautiful words in a devotional this week, they really touched my heart! I am so grateful when my heart is touched; it is the only way that I find the energy to triumph in my daily combat with depression. God's Word and inspired thoughts that are related to it, have that kind of power, the power to touch me enough to change my mind and joyfully say yes to life again, every day afresh and anew.

As life begins to wake up my heart again, the readiness rises in me to look out for proof of that beauty of God all around me. It has of course always been there, but I had forgotten to enjoy it. Suddenly I remember how deep in my heart I have always desired to demonstrate this beauty, to manifest it. It is as if an old passion in me reawakens.

All of a sudden, the way I move and walk changes. I slow down, become less hasty, less hectic. I cherish the moment, appreciate what I see.

Now I have time also, to appreciate this beautiful life at work not only around but inside me. How could I still see myself as worthless or inferior if I really knew, really "got it" in my spirit, that nothing about me is exempt from that beauty? Even the organs in my belly are beautiful and pristine. My digestive processes are beautiful. My heart is beautiful, my thoughts are beautiful, and so are the fruits I produce.

What if this beauty could be seen in my actions and interactions? What would that look like, how would it feel? Let me ponder that thought. Everything I touch is touched by God's beauty that flows through my hands and my eyes, and also my words. Does that mean I am blessing the world by being here?

You may say, hold on a minute, is that not a bit extreme, are you not a bit over the top? Believe me, the dark voice of condemnation in the mind of the depressed person is no less extreme. Meditating on the reality of who I am in Christ is God's antidote, and the doses taken have to be strong enough to lighten up the atmosphere in a mind that has been listening to lies for decades.

Besides, is it possible to overestimate what God has placed inside of us? He wants us to hold our head up high, as carriers of his nature. For love of Him, for His glory, not our own.

This beauty is always recognized because it is not of this world it is heavenly, pure and incorruptible. I recognise it because it makes me feel light and free, and others may recognise it too. It is joyful and exquisite. So, if it has something to do with me that this beauty is manifested around me, I have a part to play!

With such a calling on my life, how can my life be insignificant, how can I be depressed? Longing to be aligned with the beauty that God has given me, I am more than willing to drop all that interferes with the experience of it, all my darkness and negativity. God does not need to "wrestle" with me to change me, because I come willingly, attracted, drawn by His beauty and loving-kindness.

God's divine love in me

Now hope does not disappoint; because the love of God has been poured out in our hearts by the Holy Spirit who was given to us (Romans 5:5)

Today I enjoyed the thought that love is one of the fruits of the spirit, in other words it is a *product* of my spirit. Just then I was walking past a business that, sadly, had closed down, along with so many other Irish businesses in these recessionary times. Nothing produced anymore, their products no longer wanted. And here I walk, realizing that I have a product to offer called the love of God, derived from the activity of the Holy Spirit in me.

I am more productive than I have ever been in my life, and I need not worry that there may not be a demand for my products, because I know there is. It is true, I have reached the age where I am unlikely to produce any more children, but that does not mean that I cannot be enormously fruitful. Mixing God's Word with my faith and enthusiasm causes productivity and creativity on all kinds of levels.

If this love of God has been "shed abroad" in

my heart by the Holy Spirit (see Romans 5:5), then it is not just a speck of love, insignificant and lost among whatever else my heart might harbour. To me it means that this love is big, reaching everywhere, taking the dominion of my heart. And that is because it is alive, it is not sitting there, passive. Therefore, I cannot very well ignore it. I did not put this love there, I did not author it. But as I carry this living force in me, I am changed. It is inevitable.

If I resist its urgings and promptings, if I suppress this love, neglect to express it, try to do without it, is it any wonder I get depressed? Such a powerful presence that is alive and at work in you like a yeast; at the same time needing your cooperation and care like a baby that grows in your womb, is it any wonder that resisting it would drive you crazy?

Expressing that love, power, joy and light, that is what is natural to a child of God. Not expressing it is such a waste of this glorious treasure. Depending how sensitive someone is, they might occasionally feel a vague regret of not rising to the honour of their calling, or they might like myself feel deep sadness, and a sense of pain that cannot be shaken off.

I love God's Word, passionately. I delight myself in it, I rejoice in it; it is precious to me, I need it and could not live without it. In its presence I am well, I am whole, and my perception and consciousness are transformed. What has been limited and narrow is suddenly comfortably spacious.

Where there was no way forwards the view is now wide open with possibilities, what has been gloomy and obscure has been lit up and made clear, where there was nothing to hold on to there is new strength. How can I not cry for joy and love for the Word? This love must be divine love.

My ordinary human brain could never find anything to be excited about in God's Word. No, it is my spirit that responds to God's spirit as expressed in the scriptures, to His essence of love, freedom and power. My spirit that with a huge thrill, with a jump of joy, recognizes my kinship with Him, recognizes in fact that I am burning with love and devotion for God. This is where I am at home, in the presence of the Word.

What I really want is just stay there and adore

Him. But I guess there is more that could be done to manifest this divine love. As I meditate on it, I see myself carrying this divine love like someone would carry a baby that they are doting on. Holding it tenderly, cradling and protecting it, but also showing it happily to all the world, delighted that my darling touches the hearts of everyone we meet.

I also see myself carrying the Word with me like a tool. Like a screen, or a frame, that I place over every situation I encounter and look through it. As I look through it, I can see the situation for what it is. All the distractions are gone, and I can see the essence.

If I was listening to something, all the static would be gone, and I would have a clear reception. Another image is that of an Allen key. You can get a set of such keys in all different sizes, each key designed to be the exact right fit for a particular screw. That is how it is with the Word. It offers me the exact one and only key that will fit to loosen a stuck circumstance, a situation that could not be budged by anything else.

Ultimately, I long to be able to walk in the

consciousness of the presence of the Word and of my love and kinship with it, no matter where I am. Coming back to the image of key: nowadays, instead of a key granting us access somewhere, we are issued with a card we need to swipe. An identity card that ultimately opens the door, or the gate. God's Word is this identity card, my identity in Christ. With it I will be identified as a child of God; and thus, doors are opening.

Manifesting my love for the Word of God, also means carrying with me the certainty and conviction of its validity wherever I go. A quiet and unshakeable peace, that brings stability into my world because I do not relinquish my place in the Word and the dignity, order and privileges that naturally go with that position as a Son of God. It means manifesting my rights, my inheritance, and my blessings with ease because I do not doubt anymore who my Father is.

I love the word self-giving. I love thinking of the love of God in me being forever self-giving. Not self-hiding, out of shame and guilt, no longer self-condemning. I am no longer seeking to love you because I consider you lovable and worthy, whereas I am embarrassed of who I am, secretly undeserving of your love, worried that you might one day find out and be repelled by my true nature.

Instead, self-giving means I joyously, happily give of myself to you. I see your loveliness, and I am aware of my own loveliness too. They are not mutually exclusive anymore, and so I can give to you of myself, my love, unafraid and unperturbed like a child, knowing that I have been made "the righteousness of God" (see 2 Corinthians 5:21). And in that righteousness, there is nothing wrong: nothing wrong with me, and nothing wrong with you. And thus, we are two innocent children coming hand in hand before the Father's throne.

Letting go

The weapons of our warfare are not carnal, but mighty through God, to the pulling down of strongholds, casting down imaginations and every high thing that exalts itself against the knowledge of God, and taking captive every thought to the obedience of Christ (2 Corinthians 10:4-5)

It may seem that learning how to let go of someone is what you must do to forget somebody who used to be part of your life, for instance when a romantic relationship comes to an end. I also had to learn to let go of the pain of separation when my children and grandchildren emigrated to far away continents; or indeed when people dear to me passed away.

I must admit though that, at least in my case, letting go really is a lesson that needs to be learned at any stage of a relationship, with anyone.

Let me tell you what I learned in the area of romantic relationships. In my experience, though obsessive preoccupation with a person seems to be normal when you are in love, and it can be fun to begin with; yet I would say, may you be delivered from that glorious madness sooner rather than later.

It can be a killer of love, because love really feels good and radiant only when it is given in perfect freedom, whereas obsession and freedom are simply not compatible.

Obsessiveness is a painful experience, especially if there is something you crave, some unfinished business, something you want the other person to do or to say. You may be able to see quite clearly that this fixation is not good for you, and you may really want to let go and stop mentally circling around that person. Yet your thoughts keep gravitating towards them, it is like you are imprisoned by your own thoughts. This is an example of what the Bible calls a "stronghold".

Meditating on the above scripture, 2 Corinthians 10:4-5 has helped me again and again. Not only, because for the duration that my mind dwells on it I have escaped from my obsessive thoughts, which is a little victory in itself. Even more valuable is that what I discover brings about a more lasting relief.

First, this verse confirms that I cannot beat this thing in my own strength, but that help is available which is more effective than my little ideas about what should be done in the situation. I am wise enough to know that my own approach is what the scripture calls "carnal", and it is limited. I recognize that this obsessive thinking is a stronghold in my mind which I do not want there. It needs to be pulled down, and the scripture reassures me that it can be done.

At this point, a shift occurs in my mind. I realize that in truth I do not even want to do this to the other person, I want to leave them free to be who they are. Something in me says, give them a break; please let them off the hook. Suddenly it feels like I am actually hurting them by forcing them to be enthroned in this centre place of my mind. I have been putting quite a bit of pressure on them. Amazingly, I actually feel regret, feel like apologizing to the person.

Next, it talks about the casting down of imaginations: this is all the crazy ideas I have woven around the person. In my heart I have always known that a lot of my thoughts about them are indeed imaginations, things I picture, fantasize, and project onto them. There are many things I suspect, motives for their actions that I freely invent, interpretations and distortions which are being unjust and unfair.

These make me feel like a madwoman, and I do not like myself like that. Casting down this insane activity of my mind is another promise of this scripture to which I gladly say Yes.

"... and every high thing which exalts itself against the knowledge of God". This high thing is the thought that seemed so hot in my mind only a few minutes ago. This thing which I want of the person, which would make me feel better, which would give me some sort of peace, though I do not even really know what it is. I realize that, yes, I want this pulled down as well.

It was an insane idea which was putting an unfair demand on the other person and on the situation, purely born of the mistaken belief, that I am not okay as I am, that there is something missing, I am not complete, and it is somehow this person's fault.

Choosing the knowledge of God instead, means choosing the knowledge of who I am in

Christ. A light goes on and I remember what I really want: the peace that comes with knowing that I cannot be deprived, cannot be disadvantaged, the peace that passes all understanding (see Philippians 4:7).

Again, I feel like apologizing - for my feverish imaginations, my high expectations, all of which got in the way of seeing the person for who they are. The regret is heartfelt, because I have woken up to realizing that I would much rather experience and *enjoy* this person, who has done nothing wrong, in freedom and without the fear that made me grasp and hold on – and ultimately left me empty-handed. And once again I remember how important mind-control is, which is what is meant by "taking captive every thought".

It can be tempting to slip back into the old mental patterns, there seems to be a sick satisfaction in holding on to them, in making the other person guilty somehow, in looking for and finding reasons to feel wronged and hurt. I know, because why else am I back in that dark place so often? Yet I can choose "obedience", I can make all my thoughts submit to the truth of who I am in

Christ. To let go of someone equals removing all the blocks to the love in our hearts – what a sweet reward.

Love

And walk in love, as Christ loved us and gave himself up for us, a fragrant offering and sacrifice to God (Ephesians 5:2)

Today I was meditating on "walking in love", feeling a little pathetic in confessing that love is my nature as a child of God. My negative mind was telling me that I am kidding myself and it is ridiculous to think that I am a loving child of God.

I was hanging in there trying to remember moments of which I could say, that is when I was loving. I could not grasp it; it just was a non-reality that I could not picture with my inner eyes, in my spirit, and therefore would not be able to claim in the "natural" either. The conviction that in truth I am ugly and unable to love, was profound.

Then my miracle happened. Suddenly I remembered, the way for me to be at my most loving is when I refuse to believe any nonsense about myself. There is no need to focus on analysing myself: Am I really loving? How can I be more loving? Does such and such a person feel loved by me? Am I doing the right thing or not, am I behaving appropriately?

All I need to detect is what is blocking the way of love, insist on "taking captive every thought" that is in fact a lie about me, and refuse to identify with it (see 2 Corinthians 10:5). Instead, I simply concentrate on what God says about me, and suddenly I remember I like the person that I am in Christ.

It is the woman that does not hang on to resentment or fear, who makes it easier for others to be themselves as well, who does not entertain any secret thoughts of self-loathing and self-condemnation because she is like a child aware only of being loved by her Father.

From that mindset, love flows by itself, the love that "has been shed abroad in my heart by the Holy Spirit" (see Romans 5:5) cannot help but express itself. Love is not unlocked by "doing" (works) but by "being"; being who I am in Christ. Thank you Holy Spirit for reminding me.

Forgiveness

I have loved you with an everlasting love (Jeremiah 31:3)

There was a time in my life where I gradually became aware how often I slipped into an unforgiving mindset where I held a grudge against those around me without even knowing why. There was something I blamed them for, and I could not even put my finger on it. Like resentment was my default mode. Unfortunately, it tended to be those nearest and dearest to me that had to suffer the impact of my negativity. Something in me wanted them to pay for my unhappiness.

I was especially hard on the one I chose to be the object of my love, the special one I allowed into my heart! Because I would expect of him actual perfection. Somehow, I wanted him to give me everything that I felt others had not given me, make up for all that life had deprived me of.

I suppose I wanted to be loved with a perfect and unfailing love. So that I could feel good about myself, worthy and loveable, respected, and important – all the things that secretly I believed I was not. I did not realize how unrealistic and unfair my expectations were; and did not understand that this kind of love had already been given to me by God.

On the one hand, I was demanding that which I thought I was lacking from the significant other in my life. On the other hand, I would make it difficult for that person to do anything right. I was too bitter to actually notice and recognise the expressions of their love. Their gifts were brushed aside as insignificant or worse still, as not that which I expected or wanted.

It was only when I snapped out of my "insanity" that I was able to put myself in the shoes of the other and get an inkling of how hurtful my arrogant attitude was. And this I could not do without the help of One greater than myself.

And yet I might wake up the next morning and feel dismayed that once again my heart was closed. Resentment was back and they had done something wrong again. I asked myself, what is wrong with me, why am I so hypersensitive and forever finding fault? Why can I not *love*?

I learned that if I do not want to spend the day being pained about my own unloving behaviour, I have no choice but to ask the Holy Spirit, my inner teacher, to please help me see this differently, help me forgive the other person. I gradually came to realize that I needed to forgive them for a hurt inside of me, that they had not caused at all, an old wound in my emotional makeup for which I wanted to blame them and expected them to pay.

The long and the short of it is that in truth I did not feel worthy of the other person's love, of anyone's love, for that matter. I kept doubting their love because I was still convinced that I was not loveable. Worse and very sadly, I would sometimes take the token of their love and twist it into an offense to me. That is how deep my insanity was.

The Holy Spirit began to show me the games I play, and to stir in me sadness and regret for my actions (even if I did not act them out). Now I can truthfully tell Him, I really do not want to be like this anymore, please help me to change. It is at this point then - my heart prepared by my pain over my own unlovingness - that I am willing and eager to embrace the truth which the Holy Spirit brings to my awareness.

He brings to my remembrance all the scriptures I have meditated on, that speak about God's love for me, the experiences I have had of His glorious love, and reminds me of all that I have learned about who I am in Christ. I am as lovely as He is, I have my Father's nature, the same passionate love; the heart in my chest is His loving heart.

As I walk in love, I *cannot* be deprived, either. The gifts and blessings I receive from the hands of others are no longer lost in the bottomless void inside me. There is no scarcity, my cup is full, I meet those gifts with the fullness of my joy. I receive graciously all that adds to the beauty of my life and increases the glory that is already there.

And so, I am no longer the jealous, suspicious, discontent madwoman I thought I was. I release others from the burden of having to try and fill me up. What a relief! Suddenly I can see with my heart again. I see the expressions of their love to which I had been blind, and I also see how they are longing for mine. And all I want to do is to respond.

Like an edifice

But you, beloved, build yourselves up (founded) on your most holy faith (make progress, rise like an edifice higher and higher), praying in the Holy Spirit (Jude 1:20 AMP)

I can relate to the idea of building myself up by meditating on God's Word and praying in the Spirit. I know from experience that it energizes me and lifts me up, and this is what I need and will keep on doing!

Making progress, however, building my life like an edifice, which means a large and imposing building – sometimes I feel impatient! How do I go about manifesting the glory and power of God? How can I demonstrate, through my own example, the revolutionary realities contained in His Word? How can I live in such a way that others recognize in me "the glorious liberty of the sons of God"? Perhaps it means aiming high.

Sometimes I forget. Like that day when I went to take care of the bathrooms in the church. I thought, there is nothing monumental or imposing about my life whatsoever, no edifice here. I was feeling empty, and my life seemed to be going nowhere. Then I remembered the above scripture. "Founded on your most holy faith" - do I have faith in God's Word? Yes, I do! Is my faith holy? Yes. I love the scriptures; they are precious to me.

Then it struck me. Those scriptures are meant to be the holy building blocks of my life. Every day, every hour, every moment, if I like, I can take one of them and build it into the fabric of my life. This is how I build my edifice. I fell in love with the beauty of that thought.

So here I was, doing the bathrooms. I remembered my pastor saying that when we do a job in the church, we are not doing it for the pastors but with the awareness that we are doing it for God. I must admit that I very rarely have that awareness; my thoughts distracted and all over the place, I cannot claim that God is on my mind much when I do a physical job.

That afternoon, however, I remembered that I wanted the beauty and glory of God to be reflected in my actions; and so, I decided to make this time an offering of love to Him. I did the job with a smile and with a flourish, feeling close to God and feeling enriched and joyful. I was doing something I was meant to do, with the attitude I was meant to do it, and that felt very good. Suddenly even something unremarkable as cleaning the bathrooms could become an occasion to add another building block to my edifice.

Another thought I enjoyed was that after all, these bathrooms are used by the sons and daughters of the King. That is what we are, royalty. If we had, say, the Queen of some country visiting our church, what would we do in preparation? We might get the bathrooms painted, but in the end, it would still be the very basic facilities in our humble little church. We could not change that, but we would do our very best to make the place as presentable and neat and beautiful as possible, making the best out of what has been given us.

I have to smile now at the fact that in my self-righteousness I sometimes thought, sure, we can make do with less expensive toilet paper, no need to spend more money than absolutely necessary on that. I was wrong. Meanwhile I believe that a spirit of joy and abundance can be expressed in these little details. Anything that makes the place inviting and pleasant is justified and surely pleasing to God.

Finally, it gave me pleasure to show God, that even though our church is small and modest, our worship is no less heartfelt than that of a large affluent church, His presence is not dependent on the number of members or the luxuriousness of the venue. When we are celebrating Him, this is Heaven, and cracks in the ceiling or leaking windows are non-existent. For now, this is our home, and on a Sunday morning it is the most beautiful place on earth, and we are happy to take care of it as if it already was the splendid place that one day might become ours when it is time to move on.

Having had this experience, the quiet voice is still there, saying gently, you could make today a lovely time too, this could be a highlight of your week. You have the choice to let every activity be brim-full with joy and satisfaction. When I listen and follow, I realise the Holy Spirit is forever intent on showing me better, richer ways of living. He is forever seeking to upgrade my life. That is what it must mean to move "from glory to glory".

It is up to us whether we want to dare accept the realities He shows us or stay with our old ways of doing and seeing things.

The child inside

Beloved, I wish above all things that thou mayest prosper and be in health, even as thy soul prospereth (3 John 2)

I love it when in my quest for good feeling thoughts, a scripture which I have known and liked for many years comes to life in new ways.

God addresses me as Beloved; to know that I am beloved, that is a beautiful thought, inviting me to feel good about it. Even if often, I have a hard time believing that I am loveable, and even if at times I think I require more hands-on proof that I am loved, I can muster the willingness, the humility, to accept that nevertheless I am beloved. If I allow that possibility, ponder it with an open mind, I have to say it does feel good.

So, yes, for now I will shyly accept the truth that I am in a loving relationship, that I am the object of the loving attention and affection of the Divine.

The scripture goes on to say that God wishes for me to prosper and be in health, even as my soul prospers. I used to think, yes of course, that

179

is just like a father wishing health and prosperity for his beloved child. That is obvious, I thought.

In light of what I am learning now, there is even more to it. I like to think that God in Heaven from where I came forth into this world, is as excited about this earthly experience for me as I was when I first arrived on the planet. What if God is still as keen and eager to live this life with me, in me and through me, to the full, as I was as a toddler and as a child?

God is always with me, as I am beginning to understand. If we are in this together, then naturally we can much more fully partake in everything that life has to offer, and much more of His Spirit can be expressed through me, while I am fully healthy both in body and in my soul. So yes, this is a good reason to take good care of my body and be healthy for Him. Also, since everything the Holy Spirit does is done happily, lovingly, easily, it stands to reason that I too should be happy, loving, and at ease, so that the Holy Spirit and I are agreed and can make the most out of this earthly life.

The scripture mentions my soul: what about my soul, which I understand to mean my mind and emotions, is there wellness and happiness, does my soul prosper?

I know for definite that I had boundless enthusiasm for life as a child. However, growing up, always a good girl, I must have learned to believe, along with my family, that being excited would not get me anywhere. Being an avid learner, I adopted my well-meaning family's advice, do not expect or hope for anything good, so then you will not be disappointed. I learned to think like they did, and, starting with my teenage years, the excitement for life that once fuelled me was replaced by a life-long cloud of depression.

I grew up sadly convinced that there is not enough, not enough money, not enough time, not enough strength, not enough space for me, not enough love; there was no point wishing for anything or desiring anything because you could not have it. Deeply internalized, I continued that outlook throughout my adult years, saw evidence of it all around me, it was my truth, my reality. My parents did not know that there is another way of looking at life, and so neither did I.

You might say, over the years, my soul felt impoverished rather than prosperous.

I remember my mother having a phase in the 1980s where she was excited about positive "affirmations"; but neither she nor I seemed to be able to think the positive thoughts we were supposed to think. They proved too much of a stretch from our habitual mindsets of negativity and powerlessness. We did not seem to have the emotional strength to *feel* what we were trying to think.

Picturing what I want and visualizing what I desire certainly does feel unfamiliar when I have not done it since my early years. Nevertheless, something in me is extremely excited at the concept of creating and attracting into my life what I first see and believe in my mind's eye. It is no doubt the child in me that loves being invited to find out what I desire, even if for most of my life I have never quite known what that is.

It seemed to always have been my job to focus on what others might need or want and then go along with that. Not only that, but I rarely knew how I felt about anything either, so busy monitoring how those around me were feeling and how I could gain their approval.

Still, I realize this is not as hard to learn as I thought. The child in me, still the eager learner, and so grateful to finally have her say again, is getting the hang of this and certainly knows how she feels about things. God wants my soul to prosper, and it is like now I begin to understand what that means. Let me practice the prosperity of my soul! It is like using an underdeveloped muscle.

I am learning that it is my feelings that let me know whether I am making baby steps in the right direction or not. I do not expect spectacular progress of myself anymore, I do not have to master this and be perfect at it overnight. However, it helps me enormously when I feel I am at least on the right track, when there is a sense of relief, a slight increase in the light on the horizon. It is wonderful when I realise that what I have been thinking right now feels a little better, I am doing the right thing, and there is more where that came from.

Since I have been blessed with a vivid imagination and creativity, I am now willing to use it consciously, *for* me, rather than against me; deliberately designing in my mind little scenarios that please me, that I would like to experience. Rather than imagining problems and struggle, I use my super productive mind to create positive outcomes. It is very unfamiliar and new for me, but I realize, those happier thoughts are there, I just need to look for them and dwell on them.

I realise that what I pay attention to and focus on is what I attract and what I will have more of in my life. "As a man thinks in his heart, so is he," we are told in Proverbs 23:7. I want to concentrate on what I like in those around me; if there is something to appreciate in someone let me amplify it and look out for more; if there is something good, something positive to note about a circumstance let me claim it and find more (see Philippians 4:8).

Can my soul be "filthy rich"? Would it be wrong to prosper and be in health physically, emotionally, socially, financially, spiritually – can you overdo it, imagining too much, too high, too vivid and satisfying, too over-the-top? I think not.

Is it a crime to feel intensely the beauty of what you see in your mind's eye? Is there a health hazard attached to indulging wonderful emotions because in your imagination you have pulled out all the stops, realizing the sky is the limit, realizing there *is* no limit?

How about becoming a master at picturing and deeply enjoying the feeling of all I desire, all that I would like to have, be, or do, and realizing that I am actually attracting these things and circumstances as I think about them.

If it is true that I am meant to prosper my soul, be prosperous in my mind and emotions, and if God delights himself in my prosperity, as Scripture tells us, then I not only have permission to employ my happy imagination, then I better get on with it right away, for my life depends on it!

Thinking on purpose

No eye has seen, no ear has heard, and no mind has imagined what God has prepared for those who love him (1 Corinthians 2:9)

Yesterday I felt my mind was drifting aimlessly here and there, there was a niggling sense that I was not making very good use of it. It is the kind of passive mental attitude which leaves me feeling in the evening as if I have somehow wasted the day, like another day of my life has slipped by, and somehow, I did not make the most of it; it is the dull awareness that I did not at all live up to who I can be or want to be.

It really is a feeling of discontent that, if I allow it to go on for too long lands me in a low mood, where my mind looks for something to obsess about, or heads into the quagmire of past experiences, only to get stuck in some memory of hurt or regret and guilt.

It is in fact a dangerous state to be in as it is wide open to all kinds of negative thoughts, such as worry and pessimism about the future. It is a state of mental idleness that, as I know from decades of experience, lands me in a foggy consciousness at best and depression at worst.

Thankfully, I am becoming aware when I am heading down that road; I am learning to get a hold on my mind and think better thoughts "on purpose". So that is what I did yesterday. I took myself for a walk which for me is the best way to enjoy my own company and meditate on something that may help uplift me.

While my very active mind has the absolute potential to torment me and has done so for a large part of my life, I am beginning to be more serious about filling it with what I want, rather than with what I do not want. I have discovered I can use my mind to shape my life rather than to hurt myself with my own thoughts!

A very good anchor and starting point is God's Word. So, I turned my mind to 3 John 2:1 "Beloved, I wish that you may prosper and be in health, even as your soul prospers." What would a prosperous life look like? I know God delights himself not only in my financial prosperity, but prosperity in all areas of my life. I could bring those areas to life by thinking about them.

First of all, regarding my mind itself, what kind of thoughts would it be filled with, what kind of thoughts feel truly prosperous? I would indeed like to access the prosperity of my own mind – and often it is God's Word revealed to me by the Holy Spirit that shows me this prosperity.

I went on painting beautiful mental images for my body in prosperous health, and for my finances: what would I like to do if money was not an issue? I pictured how I would love my talents to bud and blossom and contribute to the world; and I pictured what I would consider emotional prosperity especially for my family, for us. I pictured all these areas prospering.

In other words, I have begun to explore the possibilities of putting my heart and soul into imagining my ideal life, allowing myself to feel it as if it were already so; daring to *believe* in my dream. The Bible says, "As a man thinketh in his heart, so is he" (Proverbs 23:7); and of course, "Therefore I tell you, whatever you ask for in prayer, believe that you have received it, and it will be yours" (Matthew 11:24).

As so often, I was feeling flat as I set off for my walk; I just knew I wanted to get out of that useless mental state. So, I willed myself to think about these areas and how I would love them to look. It was an hour well spent, I soon enjoyed being back in the swing of useful, meaningful thinking, and I went on having a light-hearted rest of the day.

I believe we can probably do way more than we realise by thinking and feeling "on purpose". At the same time though, I do not like to get too specific in my imaginings, I make it more about how I would like to *feel*, rather than telling God what the details of my life should be. I do believe that with all my human picturing I do not even come near what God may have in mind for me; and I will be very happy to step back and be shown.

The Holy Spirit

And they were all filled with the Holy Spirit... (Acts 2:4)

When I start my prayer with the words "Dear Father" I start off by turning to Him, I am addressing Him. I am not just talking to myself. Instead, I come home to where my Father lives, a warm place where I am always welcome. He is my Father, and I am so grateful and proud that He calls me His daughter. I come home to Him with all my love, and I know I bring Him joy by giving Him my affection.

I show Him that I mean it, that I am very sincere in what I feel for Him. It gives me such joy when I can get in touch with and express that tenderness, the depth of devotion and the sweetness that is too wide to be contained in ordinary words.

Often however, I need to make an effort before I can experience the relief and joy of casting off everything limiting and burdening and come before Him like a carefree child. Resentment or self-pity can then be like a barrier between me and

God, a hardness of heart making it seem pointless to seek His presence. At such times, if I manage to feel the sadness, the tears underneath the bitterness, this will help open and soften me enough to be ready to come home once more and be delivered from my heavy dream.

Having started off like that I thank Him, really thank Him, for His Holy Spirit dwelling in me. I know I am even at the best of times only dimly aware of all that He blesses me with every day of my life. I am a long way from expressing my gratitude appropriately. Yet of late He seems to draw my attention increasingly to the fact that the indwelling presence of the Holy Spirit is the greatest gift of all.

It is of such inestimable value that our minds can barely understand it; but even if I am only vaguely able to appreciate the hugeness of this gift, I know that thanks are due. I am eager to let Him know that I am not dismissing His gift, that I know that without it I would be hopelessly lost. I do my best to express my gratitude that by giving me His Spirit He Has opened all doors for me and has made nothing impossible for me; because nothing is impossible for Him who now lives in me.

I long to embrace as real what the Holy Spirit's presence in my life means; what He offers, holds out to me, waiting patiently for me to wake up and say yes to. He works like a yeast in my life, forever active and seeking to expand it. I think what happens is that He causes a gradual change in my consciousness which He shows me in images as I meditate.

He is like a sharp presence in my life, that cuts and blazes away everything that is sick, deathlike, heavy. He straightens and makes upright what was twisted, lopsided or limp and juiceless in me. He opens windows in my life and lets in fresh air and light in an area where I had only seen a dead end, and so often, He *widens* my vision; delivers me from the narrowness that was near enough choking the life out of me.

He keeps on widening paths that I had given up upon, convinced there was no way forward due to the obstacles on all sides. He is having none of that, He is so eager to show me and convince me that it is true that all things have become new. Behold!

This evening I was battling an attack of fear. How to describe it? A nameless dread, a terror at something I cannot even put my finger on, brought on by something one of my grown-up kids was engaging in, a vague expectation of something catastrophic going to happen before long. It is an irrational fear that makes me go numb and helpless, like I am catapulted back into a time, not too many years ago, where this consciousness was very much part of my everyday experience.

As I go for a walk in the fresh air, I do my best to focus on thanking God for "bringing me into the glorious liberty of the Sons of God".

Gradually, in the space of about 45 mins, does the knot begin to loosen, I begin to see God's compassion for my suffering, bringing me out of the darkness, out of bondage, into His Kingdom, where no evil spirit can lord it over me anymore. I remember He did that because He loves me. He wants me in His family.

The liberty He has brought me into is not liberty as the world defines it. It is the *glorious* liberty of the Sons of God, a liberty that reflects

His glory, His wholeness and fullness. A wholesome freedom, that contains all that befits a child of God; and suddenly a little memory stirs of what the Holy Spirit has begun to show me, the promises, the things that my Father has prepared for those who love Him.

I begin to defrost, no longer paralyzed with dread. I am alive enough to remember my heart's desire, my dreams. I am back! And another victory has been won over one of my demons. Hallelujah!

It is true, now I am free to sing and dance for Him in praise. The oppression was stealing my joy. Of course it is not easy to jump for joy when you feel oppressed. Or raise your arms when you feel worthless; but what else would you want to do when you have been released from an ancient old fear? I think the more you have been imprisoned, the greater is the joy and thrill of liberty; the darker it has been, the more radiant will be your praise.

In your presence

You will show me your path of life: in your presence is fullness of joy; at your right hand there are pleasures for ever more (Psalm 16:11)

I was driving home from the airport. There was no denying that saying goodbye left me feeling deflated. While it is natural to feel like that for a while, I knew I had to be careful not entertain these emotions too much. I reminded myself that Scripture says, in God's presence there is fullness of joy. Where was the joy now?

Would I suddenly have fallen out of His presence, cut off from it because I had indulged in feelings of resentment and self-pity? I knew that those negative emotions can seriously get in the way of experiencing the presence of God. Of course, I knew that I myself was the sole reason for my joyless state, and I wanted to get out of that mindset and back into the sunshine.

I have always loved the above scripture about the fullness of joy that can be found in God's presence. And even dwelling on His Word is a way of interrupting the negative chatter and for my thoughts to be elevated. It is a way of entering into His presence.

Yet my resistance was strong. I began reasoning with myself: my being in God and God in me, does not depend on outer circumstances. He has not gone away somewhere and abandoned me. His presence in me and all around me does not increase and diminish, only my awareness of it does! He is not gone missing; I am the one that is asleep.

Surely the joy in His presence is always full, and it is up to me whether I can embrace it, feel it, rejoice and delight myself in it, or not. There is nothing outside of me that determines how full my joy can be, how much I am allowed today. There is nothing whatsoever withholding any of it or preventing me from reaching all the way to bliss even.

If I do not feel any of it, is it not because I am unwilling, because something seems more important, or more enticing? In this case it was a little resentment that I wanted to wallow in for a bit; also, a worry that I thought needed to be dwelt upon and examined from all sides; and there were feelings of abandonment and loneliness, with a voice calling for a pity party that seemed justified.

Meanwhile I was surrounded by a thousand blessings, but I did not see them; the joy of the Lord, the fullness of joy, was all around me, quietly and patiently waiting for me to get over my fit of madness and return to it. Waiting to envelop me again, once I allowed it. Even there in the car on the motorway. That is when I found the willingness to say thank you.

You could say it was by grace that I managed to snap out of my mood. As I decided to feel gratitude my eyes landed on a delightful pink truck with beautiful red writing on it; and I spontaneously thought, how very sweet, how very nice – thank you.

I became aware of the pleasure of driving my car, the miracle of being transported swiftly along over the smooth surface of the road, while all I had to do was hold the steering wheel, with absolutely no effort. It was like I experienced the joy of driving, and I imagine it must be something like this a toddler feels when they ride their first tricycle; or what the inventors of the first cars felt.

I have felt that driver's delight before, and there is no reason not to re-feel it!

At the same time the radio was playing the most exquisite classical music and I felt the sound system in the car was so wonderfully excellent. I could hear so many layers of the music, the voices of the different instruments, and I felt gratitude not only for the total luxury of this entertainment on my journey, but for being able to *enjoy* it. Feeling my feelings is precious, feeling anything at all is not something easily available when you are in a state of depression. I enjoyed the programme, and that meant I was *alive*. Thank you.

Finally, there was the traffic around me. There was nobody in a rush, no impatient fast drivers – instead, everyone seemed at their ease. I was aware of a small car now behind me, now before me; we overtook each other every so often. On the whole, we were agreed on the same speed. You might say, we flowed easily with each other, the participants of the traffic in general were all in a peaceful flow; or so at least it seemed to me. We were all on our way and it was lovely.

I was content, and that is because I was back in the present moment. I believe God's presence can only be experienced in the present moment. I was back in His presence, and I had my joy back. It was a quiet joy: after all I was driving a motor vehicle; but it was enough. There was enough "fullness of joy", I had my fill, I did not feel I needed any more.

And yet, my friends, at times I get an inkling, a hunch, of the possibility of still much more joy. At times it feels as though we need to *dare* to delight ourselves in all that only seems so ordinary! It is like we are only at the very beginning of what it could be like to be jubilant, to shout for joy, not just in church but even in our everyday life, even while we still walk this earth.

Something good

Now may the God of hope fill you with all joy and peace in believing, that you may abound in hope by the power of the Holy Spirit (Romans 15:13)

A favourite teacher of mine used to say that hope is the expectation of something good to happen. I believe something good is going to happen to me! I can hardly wait to see what God is going to do in my life today.

By His grace I might be able to capture the minds and hearts of forty-eight tourists in my care today. There may be a couple in my group who have not spoken much to each other, yet on my tour they may rediscover how much they have to share. Somebody consumed with bitterness might find that Ireland is the magical country where they can just drop and forget all that pain.

Or what if somebody stressed and deeply distrustful of being cheated and mistreated finds that the world is a good place after all, and they are with an exceptionally nice group of people on this tour? This sort of things would be my heart's desire for the people I accompany around Ireland for a few days.

I may find myself overcoming a limitation today, God may encourage me to jump over a hurdle, cause me to break through a wall. I cannot wait to see what fear He will nudge me to finally once and for all put behind me. I may rise from the "ashes of depression" and, by His grace, I may be able to cheer up someone and inspire them to throw off their own limitations.

I cannot wait to see who He will send across my path today, or into my mind. I may connect with someone today who I thought was out of reach, I may feel a oneness with them, a kinship, and it will make me happy. Or I might bury an old resentment today which I was not even aware I was carrying around with me. By His grace I might be reconciled with someone. Or with the whole world.

He may send me to the right place at the right time just when the sun breaks through the clouds and I notice its warmth on my cheek or on my back. I may perceive with gratitude the soft unpolluted air that is mine to breathe, the sounds of all manner of birds, the peaceful sight of the landscape, the countryside through which I walk.

As if my eyes have been miraculously touched, I might suddenly be enchanted by the sight of the light reflecting beautifully on the honey-coloured timber of my staircase or by the fascinating patterns in my cat's soft fur.

I might hear the still small voice inside and actually take the time to sit down and listen to a piece of music or to call somebody on the phone. I might make somebody's day and on the other hand I could be deeply touched today by somebody else's kindness, honesty or trust in me.

I might get some much-needed work done today and do it graciously, without effort or frustration but with a flourish and with joy. I might give two euros to a busker today and be happy that we shared a smile, or I might create something beautiful. Who knows, I might make a giant step on my life's journey, I might learn to trust and let go. By myself I could stay stuck, but as He goes with me, nothing is impossible.

In closing

I would like to say thank you for being my reader and agreeing to get on board my various trains of thoughts with me!

If there was anything in my articles that stirred something in you and helped to brighten your day, I would love it and be very grateful if you could put that into words and leave it as a review on Amazon.

God bless you.

Carla Eckhorst

Printed in Great Britain
by Amazon

24228935R00116